The California Bungalow

The California Bungalow

by Robert Winter
with a foreword by David Gebhard

California Architecture and Architects, Number I
David Gebhard, editor

Hennessey & Ingalls, Inc.   Los Angeles   1980

Library of Congress Cataloging in Publication Data

Winter, Robert
    The California Bungalow.

    (California architecture and architects; no. 1)
    1. Bungalows—California.   I. Title.   II. Series.
NA7571.W56   728.3'73'09794   80-14078
ISBN 0-912158-85-9

Manufactured in the United States of America.
Designed by James Marrin.
Composition and makeup by
Project Publishing & Design, Inc.

Published by
Hennessey & Ingalls, Inc.
10814 West Pico Boulevard
Los Angeles, California 90064

Contents

Foreword

The turn-of-the-century California bungalow moved in remarkable fashion through the worlds of popular and high culture. In the hands of a few gifted professional California architects—Charles and Henry Greene, Arthur and Alfred Heineman or Louis Christian Mullgardt—it became a serious architectural artifact—an artifact with which an East Coast or Midwestern architect of the time could feel comfortable. But the popular, low cost California bungalow was regarded as something else. It was almost always ridiculed by the Eastern architectural establishment. The reasons for this are easy to understand. The spirit, if not the fact, of these bungalows was that they were a non-professional, do-it-your-self product. The hundreds of small builders' bungalows which came to line the streets of Los Angeles, Pasadena and elsewhere throughout California suggested that any middle class citizen who knew one end of a hammer from the other could put the whole thing together and furthermore could build the furniture needed within and plan and plant the gardens which surrounded the dwelling.

Obviously any designed building which suggested that the polished learnedness of an architect was not needed would evoke a few reservations, especially within a profession which at the turn of the century was very much "on the make." In the first place, as Robert Winter has pointed out, these houses were not for the elite but rather for the middle and artisan classes of American society. Traditionally, architectural imagery had had its inception

at the top of the social ladder and then slowly percolated down to the middle and lower classes. The California bungalow seemed to imply that this natural God-given process had been reversed. Put in the terms of the time, the popular California bungalow was too "democratic." It suggested far too much egalitarianism.

Another disquieting quality was the sentiment, often mushy, which came to surround it. "It is 'homey,' and comes near to that ideal you have seen in the dreamy shadows of night when lying restless on your couch you have yearned for a haven of rest"—so wrote the author of *Radford's Artistic Bungalows* in 1911.[1] For a recent American graduate of the Ecole des Beaux Arts in Paris, or for an architectural practitioner who wished to be thought of as a down to earth member of the practical business community, such effusive sentimentality could produce only embarrassment.

The final misgiving about the popular California bungalow had to do with its place of origin. Any American who had been properly educated knew that the well-spring of American culture was to be found in the Northeast. The Midwestern pretenses of Chicago, Kansas City and Minneapolis were bad enough, but how could a major architectural mode flourish and be exported from distant California, let alone Southern California and Los Angeles, a remote geographic locale, which even in 1910 was suspect. "Probably the fact that the bungalow was first produced in the West, and in Southern California has been produced in its best estate, has led Eastern architects to be a little snobbish about it," noted the editor of the professional San Francisco journal, *The Architect and Engineer*. "They like to remain ignorant of something which, if not created, was at least brought to its highest expression of architectural style by their colleagues in the West."[2]

Though the popular California bungalow did indeed represent, as Gustav Stickley frequently noted in the pages of the *Craftsman* magazine, a high point of the American Arts and Crafts movement, it also came to capture certain qualities which were specifically Southern California. It was none other than Charles Sumner Greene who in 1915 observed, "In fact, between the automobile mania and the bungalow bias, there seems to be a psychic affinity . . . They have developed side by side at the same time, and they seem to be the expression of the same need or desire, to be free from the common place of convention."[3] Do-it-your-selfism and back-to-naturism, set to a new free life style embracing the autombile—these sum up the spirit of the California bungalow, and in the end Southern California.

David Gebhard
Santa Barbara

Notes

1. William A. Radford, *Radford's Artistic Bungalows,* (The Radford Architectural Co., Chicago, 1911), p. 3.
2. "Bungling the Bungalow—An Eastern Criticism," *The Architect and Engineer,* Vol. 29, July, 1912, p. 84.
3. Charles Sumner Greene, "Impressions of Some Bungalows and Gardens," *The Architect,* Vol. 10, December, 1915, p. 252.

In the Land of the Bungalow

By
GEORGE F. DEVEREAUX

A - way to the set - ting sun, _____ To the

home of the or-ange blos - som, _____ To the land of fruit and

hon-ey, Where it does not take much mon -ey, To own a lit - tle Bun - ga -

low _____ In the low. _____

RAYNER, DALHEIM & CO.
MUSIC PRINTERS
CHICAGO

Preface

Why write a book on bungalows? I realize that they have rarely been the best architecture, but almost always they have provided a comfortable abode *in style* for the average person. In that sense, they are revolutionary in the history of architecture. And I must admit a personal interest. When I was teaching at UCLA, I participated in a University Extension course called "The Pathology of the Popular Arts." I found myself saying at the end of a lecture on the bungalow and its extension into the Cape Cod cottage and the ranch house:

With a little more status and a little more dough

I'm going to buy me a bungalow!

I did and am better for it.

My first thought was to write about bungalows everywhere in the United States. As a matter of fact, there are acres of them in every North American city and village that had an economic boom in the early twentieth century. This observation includes Canada, where Vancouver has perhaps the largest collection of bungalows outside of Los Angeles. Australia is infested with them. But the real home of the bungalow is California, particularly Southern California. The one-story, single-family dwelling of that period was almost always called a "California Bungalow" wherever it was built. In its conception, the bungalow suggested California—its style of life, its mild climate, its casual living with nature. Thus, while I will not neglect bungalows in other parts of North America, my focus will be on the California development, which is central to an understanding of the American phenomenon. I have no doubt that other scholars will expand the story as well as correct my mistakes. This is certainly not the last word on bungalows. More needs to be written on style and intention as well as on bungalow courts and gardens, particular architects, and the economics of mass-produced bungalows. But I hope that my book does something to establish the concept of the bungalow before it disappears like the passenger pigeon.

My book is very strongly pictorial. In trying to put the reader in the mood of the times, I have used early photographs as often as possible. Unfortunately, bungalow books do not photograph very well and neither do the periodicals, such as the *Craftsman*, which took up the California bungalow as a cause. Excellent files of architectural photographs, such as the Los Angeles Title Insurance Company's collection, which is now housed in the Wilshire headquarters of the California Historical Society, are significantly unproductive of pictures of bungalows—not, I believe, because of photographers' distaste for the genre, but because they wanted to impress their clientele with the most expensive buildings, ones that showed economic progress. The marvelous collection at the Los Angeles County Museum of Natural History is only a little less disappointing in the matter of bungalows. I have thus (infrequently) put into my book recent photographs, usually my own, which often show the remodeled bungalow, especially with white paint, surrounded by a density of foliage which probably transcends the fondest dreams of the original builder.

Where I have taken photographs from publications, Christopher Tschoegl has been my chief artist, often bringing out more contrast than the original illustration presented. Lloyd Stone also contributed to the reproduction of "flat work." I have tried to recognize architectural photographers' original work in credits at the end, but I have undoubtedly erred in some cases where the photograph has simply turned up without identification. I would like to thank Jean Sedillos for her thoughtful suggestions while editing the text.

For photographs, but principally for ideas and inspiration, I am, as always, indebted to my friend and constant coauthor, David Gebhard. He knows as much about the bungalow as he knows about Victorian and Modern architecture—and that is much—but he has conveniently deferred and allowed me to write the first book to be listed in card catalogs under my name alone, though he is the watchful editor of the series in which it appears and has thrown an enormous amount of his own research my way.

How is it possible to thank Anthony King for his support and guidance as well as his hard-won photographs? We look forward to his social history of the European bungalow which will appear shortly. I also remember with pleasure the fine afternoon I spent touring Vancouver with Deryck Holdsworth, who is the authority on the Canadian bungalow. Indeed, it is one of the joys of life that the people who have the deepest respect for the bungalow are most generous with their time and knowledge.

They include also: Tim Andersen, John Beach, Ralph Bond, Sara Boutelle, Robert Butte, John Chase, Laura Chase, William Cross, William Current, Dianne Feinberg, Leslie Heumann, Esther McCoy, Randell Makinson, James and Janeen Marrin, Keith Marston, William Mason, John Merritt, Carol and Kennon Miedema, John Miller, Richard Mouck, Tom Owen, the Pasadena Cultural Heritage Program, especially the Survey Team, Marvin Rand, Barry Sanders, Ann Scheid, Julius Shulman, Willis Stork, Janann Strand, Geri Sullivan, Brian Thomas, and Barry Zarakov.

Otherwise, my inspiration has been the bungalow itself. As a child I lived in one in Elkhart, Indiana. I remember it as a house whose small spaces accommodated a convenient and pleasant way of life. After years of living in two-story houses of every description, I finally got a job at Occidental College and settled into a college-owned bungalow in Eagle Rock. After a few years I went up the hill to a larger one with a view. Now I live in a glorified Pasadena bungalow touched by art and history. It is good to come home.

Robert Winter
Pasadena
November 1979

Parsons House, Arthur S. Heineman (Alfred Heineman, assoc.), 1909; 1605 E. Altadena Drive, Altadena. This house has recently been moved from the southeast corner of Los Robles and California in Pasadena and is being restored. (California Historical Society/Title Insurance and Trust Co. [L.A.], Collection of Historical Photographs)

Backgrounds

Woodrow Wilson once said that Warren Gamaliel Harding was "bungalow-minded," alluding to the fact that Harding rarely thought very much about anything besides poker and the stock market. This description of Harding's mental capacity suggests that by the twenties—ironically, the greatest period of bungalow building—the term was already being used in a pejorative sense. The bungalow mania, for so it was, which pervaded the popular and professional literature of the early twentieth century was beginning to wane, especially among snobs like Wilson. By the twenties the one- or one-and-a-half-story structure that had swept across the country in the period before the Great War was losing its claim to being architecture. The popular journals gradually dropped even the word, though they continued to picture "cottages" and, much later, ranch houses, both types clearly derived from the bungalow idea. In the twenties "tasteful homes" were more often elegant two-story period revivals. Taste once more became the property of the rich, and so it has remained to the present time when no architectural publication would illustrate a house costing less (one hesitates to quote a figure in this period of inflation!) than $150,000 except as an anomaly probably created by some counter-culture crank.

In its hey-day the bungalow, costing anywhere from $500 to $5,000, was admired as "a simple but artistic" home for people of modest means.[1] "Simple but artistic"—the phrase comes up again and again in the *apologia pro vita bungalosa*, even when the rendering appears to most eyes now (and I suspect then) to be considerably heavier on the simplicity than on the artistry. But it was the idea that simplicity and artistry could be in harmony that was central to the bungalow's popularity.

Only rarely in all of history has architecture been found outside the realm of the "rich, the few, and the well-born." In the Renaissance the banking Fuggers built their so-called "Fuggerei" at Augsburg as an ideal community

Fuggerei, early sixteenth century; Augsburg, Germany. Damaged during World War II and rebuilt.

Blaise Hamlet, John Nash, 1811; near Bristol, England.

where artisans might live simply but beautifully. Similarly in 1811 a rich English Quaker, wanting to provide an artistic, even picturesque, village for his servants, employed John Nash to design "Blaise Hamlet" near Bristol. And there are other instances of the rich nobly condescending to the idea that the working man deserved to live in style. But the bungalow craze, with its bally-hoo and commercialism, was a popular movement, inspired by the popular imagination. Many Americans wanted to live simply and artistically and set out to do that. Thus the multitude of bungalows in every city and town.

During the bungalow craze, most people were probably not interested in the actual bungalow style except to know that it was there. Behind the word *artistic* was, I believe, a more profoundly realized concept—respectability. The bungalow, with all of its special features of style, convenience, simplicity, sound building, and excellent plumbing, provided respectability in an age which popularized that concept. The fact that the bungalow was a single-family dwelling set in its own lawn, if not rose garden, reinforced this image—Broadacre City without the acre. It is surely significant that the bungalow thrived in the period of Chautauqua; the rise of Women's Clubs (often housed in bungalows); and Progressive democracy with its Australian ballot, initiative, referendum, recall, and direct election of senators. In this climate of "The People, Yes!" the bungalow filled more than the need for shelter. It provided psychic fulfillment of the American Dream.

Naturally the bungalow had its prosaic, practical side. One writer noted that the period 1900–20 was one when Americans were on the move both physically and economically. To them the bungalow was a useful dwelling but one which was only temporary until they could build a more substantial and pretentious home.[2] But even this

Dutch Colonial bungalow, ca. 1910; 219 E. Columbia, Falls Church, Virginia. (Barry Zarakov)

Ebell Club, 1904; (Los Angeles County Museum of Natural History).

Tent bungalow, location probably Altadena.

Bungalow with Oriental and Swiss details, ca. 1905; 201 N. Avenue 66, Highland Park

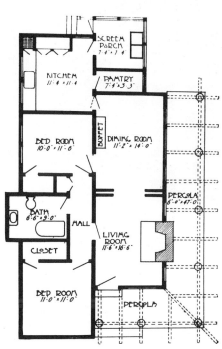

Bungalow and plan, almost certainly Arthur S. Heineman (Alfred Heineman, assoc.), ca. 1910; Standard Building Investment Company [bungalow book], p. 8.

Overleaf: Keyes House, 1911; 1337 E. Boston, Altadena. An "airplane" bungalow, named for its wingspread.

down-to-earth explanation of the popularity of the bungalow has a deeper meaning: As a half-way house it symbolized hope in a period when upward social and economic mobility was expected even if not always attained.

An even more imaginative student of the times associated the popularity of the bungalow with the rise of the city. As land increased in value, more and more people experienced the necessity —perhaps only temporary—of living in flats, apartments usually on one floor. They saw the convenience of such living and enjoyed it. At the same time they longed for the detached, single-family dwelling historically affirmed by individualistic democracy—the rural, small-town America of the nineteenth century. The bungalow was thus ideal in adapting the older America to the new.[3]

Probably the writer was exaggerating the number of Americans who had had the experience of moving from an apartment to a bungalow, but the real hitch in her argument is that while she noted correctly the dramatic rise in land values with the growth of the city, she did not comment on the fact that the bungalow, for the number of people it housed, was probably the most expensive form of shelter that could be constructed in such circumstances. Being mostly on one floor, it took even more land than a two- or three-story apartment or single-family house which had the same square-footage. Her reasoning needs to be complemented with an observation often made by other writers that the development of bungalow tracts depended upon efficient and constantly expanding public transportation systems. The bungalow was, after all, a suburban type, built in outlying areas not strongly affected by urbanization

and thus without inflated property values. It was only in such "streetcar suburbs" and "auto suburbs" that the bungalow could be built and the dreams fulfilled.

What I have been tracing so far are the advantages that California, especially Southern California, had to encourage the proliferation of the bungalow. Los Angeles and its vicinity had real estate promoters interested in transportation; Henry E. Huntington with his Pacific Electric Company and other rail systems was only the most famous of them. Southern California also had a fascination with the automobile, which in a later day would, by design, obliterate Huntington's monument, one of the finest public transportation systems in America. Relatively inexpensive land, often divided into lots with the customary fifty-foot frontage, was plentiful. A great many people in the region were on the make financially and found the simple but artistic bungalow to be at least a temporary haven in the status drive.

Southern California was the last place in America where thousands of people could have their snug little homes with their books and inglenooks and their little gardens with climbing roses and bougainvillea bringing them close to nature.

Among the shrubbery and shade trees
The brisk little bungalow stands,
Its swinging white gate speaking welcome
While its dignified doorhook commands.

Its windows so clear and so gleaming
Look out with suggestions of pride,
The walls neatly shingled and beaming
Speak well for the cosy inside.

Here neighborly spirits shine clearly
And family life is implied
From the smoke of the brick-built Dutch chimney
To the billowy curtains inside.

Here the home of American manhood
Independent and true in his life
With a welcome for friends and for neighbors
To share with his children and wife.[4]

Notes

1. See R.A. Briggs, "Bungalows," *Studio*, III (April 1894): 20, for the English expression of the idea. George A. Clark expresses it explicitly in his "Bungalow Architecture from a Layman's Viewpoint," *House Beautiful*, 24 (October 1908): 103; so does Florence Williams in "The Southern California Bungalow—a Local Problem in Housing," *International Studio*, 30 (January 1907): lxxvii.
2. Henry H. Saylor, *Bungalows* (Philadelphia: The John C. Winston Company, 1911), p. 20.
3. Warfield Webb, "Why Bungalows Are So Popular," *Keiths Magazine on Home Building* (hereafter *Keiths*), 33 (April 1915): 246.
4. "The Bungalow," *Keiths*, 33 (April 1915): 257.

California Takes Command

The bungalow was not a California invention, and, contrary to popular impression, Charles and Henry Greene, the Pasadena architects who turned out several fine bungalows, were only slightly involved in the paternity.[1] The bungalow idea was a European, probably an English, invention of the seventeenth century. Its etymological root was *bangala*, a Bengali word referring to the typical native dwelling of that region of India as well as to the region itself.[2] By the eighteenth century the Europeans had improvised upon the hut to better adapt it to their way of life. But whatever the improvisations on the original type, it remained a one-story building with a porch or "verandah," a word which seems to have originated in Persia—suggesting that the European bungalow was eclectic, a tradition which was also to mark its development in the next century. The English used variations on the *bangala*, related also to the English "cottage," as accommodations for themselves and other foreigners who traveled about India but certainly had no intention of going native. In fact, even today the term *bungalow* as used in India indicates a building in a private compound. More importantly, in India the bungalow had already developed the image of a simple dwelling, but one containing all the possible conveniences of civilization, that is, *Western* civilization.[3]

Anthony King is the most authoritative scholar of the early history of the bungalow. His two articles in the *Architectural Association Quarterly* (1973) note that, while the word is of Bengali origin, the type of building eventually developed by the British was an amalgamation of several different Indian house types as well as the British army tent.[4] People with a special interest in the simple house would do well to read King's history, though they should be warned that the buildings referred to in the nineteenth century as bungalows were not always simple. A more important point made by King is that whatever their size or style, bungalows were always considered nonurban, even when built in or near a city.[5] Their various European and

Guest bungalow, ca. 1910; at the residence of the governor of Maharashtra, Malabar Point, Bombay, India. Early twentieth century but typical of nineteenth century developments. (India Office, London)

"Dak" bungalow, 1847; lower Himalayas. (India Office, London)

Asian features were almost always associated with a symbolic return to the simple life. From the first, the English bungalow was a retreat from the society around it. As King notes, in India the bungalow,

situated sufficiently away from indigenous settlement . . ., formed a temporary base for the study and admiration of local monuments. . . . Located on a hill-top in the lower Himalayas, it provided a respite from the summer heat of the plains, a haven in the developing "hill stations" where immigrant families enjoyed their culturally preferred tastes of riding,

shooting, music, reading and, with the advantage of the specially chosen site, admiring the landscape.[6]

The later bungalow as developed in England and America was equally rural, at least in implication, and it often carried the same heavy weight of intellectual pretension. It might not have a view of the Himalayas (the San Gabriel Mountains were a good substitute!). Rarely was it the seat from which one rode to hounds. But it was an idealized country place (in miniature), a house set in a garden where culture might be nurtured in idea, if not in reality.

In spite of the Westernization of the Indian house types, certain characteristics of the Indian origin remained,

The Isaac Tolman Judson family (ca. 1920) posing proudly in front of their bungalow in Orland, California.

Bungalow, R.A. Briggs, ca. 1890; at Bellagio (now Dormans Land), Surrey, England, (Robert Thorne). Brigg's Bungalows and Country Residences (1891) was instrumental in popularizing the bungalow in England.

particularly the centrality of the living room, around which were distributed spaces for other functions. The English improved upon this idea, adding bedrooms and sometimes bathrooms on the periphery, but the idea was obviously Indian. Also, the bungalow's openness, with ventilation offered by porches almost entirely surrounding the living space, was another Indian contribution translated into English.

It was this simple house which the English built for colonial administrators throughout the empire. In England by the late nineteenth century, variations on the bungalow were being built to be used as second homes at seaside resorts and rural retreats. In 1894 R. A. Briggs, an English bungalow designer, wrote that it was "an artistic little dwelling cheaply but soundly built, with a proper regard to sanitation, and popped down in some pretty little spot, with just sufficient accommodation for our own particular needs . . . a homely, cozy little place with verandahs, balconies, oriels, and bay windows, while the plan is so arranged as to ensure complete comfort with a feeling of rusticity and ease; a place where Herrick might have sung.
Here, here I live with what my board
Can with the smallest cost afford;
Here we rejoice because no rent
We pay for our poor tenement
Wherein we rest, and never fear
The landlord or the usurer.[7]

Exactly how the concept of the bungalow as a retreat reached America has not been precisely determined. It must have come through literature and travel. At any rate, Clay Lancaster in his pioneering article on the history of the American bungalow in *Art Bulletin* (1958) found the first application of the term to an American building in the *American Architect and Building News* in 1880.[8] Significantly, the building was a summer place on Cape Cod. The next mention of it that I have found is in A. W. Brunner's *Cottages or Hints on Economical Building* published in 1884. As a matter of fact, the inclusion of the bungalow, designed by Brunner himself, in a book of "cottages"

Bungalow, ca. 1900; Sri Lanka. (Cassatt Griffin)

Typical English bungalow of early twentieth century; Moreton in Marsh, Cotswolds.

Perspective · Sketch · of · · · · ·
· · · · · · · Bungalow · (with Attic)
· Arnold · W · Brunner · Archt.   (See Plate 17)
· · · · · NEW · YORK · · · · · · ·

Bungalow from A.W. Brunner's
Cottages or Hints on Economical
Building *(1884). Frontispiece and Plate*
XVII. Notice that an owner of this
book has marked in simplifications of
the design.

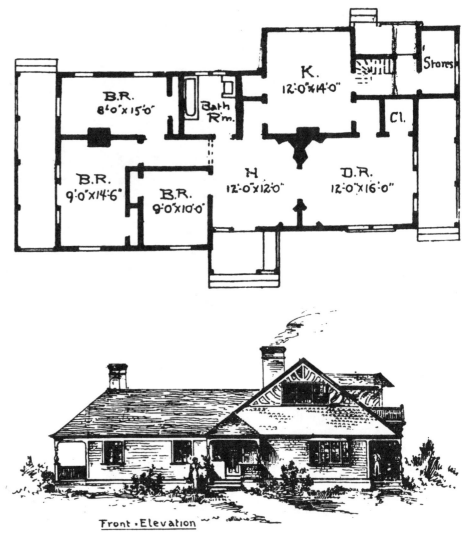

Front · Elevation

confirms Lancaster's thesis that the American bungalow grew out of the cottage idea and, as in England, was connected with a desire to find relief from the nastiness of the industrial-technological civilization.[9] Also significant is the fact that Brunner found it unnecessary to explain what a bungalow was, presumably because he believed that everyone understood the term.

Brunner's bungalow is a charming Queen Anne cottage with plenty of porches and an attic, the forerunner of the "upper room" so characteristic of the later California bungalow. Also premonitory is the fact that the entrance is directly into the living room (labeled "Hall" in the English manner), which is connected by an arch to the dining room. There is no parlor. That the kitchen is somewhat larger than the living room can only be an expression of American domestic values. Citing the advantage of living mainly on one floor, Brunner directly connected his bungalow and other cottages to a reform in architecture: "Simplicity, elegance and refinement of design are demanded, and outward display, overloading with cheap ornamentation, is no longer in favor" and he added, "now that English gables and dormers have spread so widely, now that we realize the beauty of our own colonial architecture, and that the Queen Anne craze is subsiding, so that only its best features remain, the less ambitious dwellings must not be left to the mercy of those builders whose ideas of beauty are limited to scroll-saw brackets and French roofs." He, indeed, hoped that his book would inspire those who wanted "inexpensive homes which shall be at the same time cozy and picturesque."[10]

The bungalow was with us and spread rapidly through the land in an age when simple building, especially when associated with high thinking and a celebration of nature, was very popular. Two modern German critics have written:

Bungalow, though a word often derided by professionals as inappropriate and merely fashionable, has come to represent, for many of our contemporaries, the concept of a distinct longing. It is an expression of a need for rest, of a return to Nature, of a protection from the wearing side-effects of modern technology. And finally, of the fulfillment of a desire to live, undisturbed, as an individual. . . .

Today everyone understands the word to mean the one-story detached house of modern conception which allows man, through the utilization of modern technology, to live in comfort, protected from cold, heat, rain, storm and noise, close to nature.

Naturally, the pre-requisites, as also the traditional and other local characteristics, are different in each country. But the basic idea of the modern bungalow is everywhere the same: it is the essence of all these ideas and desires, expressed in a modern and technically perfect form.[11]

The authors are talking about the northern European bungalow, but they could not have expressed the idea of the California bungalow more precisely.

Why should California literally be the reference point for the bungalow in America? Clay Lancaster has suggested that the popularity of this type in California was the result of the state's having better architects than most areas of the country. Slightly less dubious is his suggestion that Californians have always been more innovative than other Americans. But he gets at the proverbial kernel of truth when he suggests that it is the climate that brought bungalows into prominence.[12] Expand the word *climate* beyond its usual meaning and you have all the ideas and desires expressed in the foregoing quotation—everything and more, because the bungalow appeared at a time when California was the object of a migration for which the bungalow was ready-made. In the first decade of the century, in spite of wild land speculation, property was relatively inexpensive. Almost everyone could buy a small piece of land. The mild weather, of course, allowed the builder

to make economies in materials and structure so that very modest but convenient dwellings could be provided for less than one thousand dollars—at least so the advertisements said. What could be more attractive to the winter visitor, rich or poor, than to rent or buy a place in the sun! The health-seekers, some of them very ill, had cheap and easy access to California's recuperative powers. Young married couples found that even if they were not well-off, they could still afford a respectable home and garden. And the old—what attractions the homey bungalow had for them! Anthony King has phrased it well:

The bungalow, as a one-story building, had many advantages and no disadvantages. It saved the labor of servants and also that of the occupants, particularly in climbing stairs; invalids in wheel-chairs had access to all the rooms; neither children nor adults could fall on stairs; removal of furniture up and down stairs was avoided; loss of life by fire was avoided as occupants could climb out of the windows; there was security from the spread of fire as walls of rooms were carried up to the roof; gas, water and bell wires could be laid and removed more easily; soil and water pipes could not leak and damage ceilings and walls; from an architectural viewpoint, it was easier to proportion rooms as there was no upper-story to consider.[13]

The bungalow was practical, and it also symbolized for many the best in the good life. As easterners came west, they found bungalows waiting for them, either to rent for a few months, or more often to call home. And they built more. In fact, the great sprawl of the city of Los Angeles is as much testimony to the popularity of the simple little house set in its garden as it is to the fad of the automobile, which itself is a kind of extension of the single-family dwelling. The bungalow contributed to the privacy considered sacred by the middle class. The feeling of independence it gave, even on a tiny plot of land, is part of the freedom which even today one senses in Southern California.

Bungalow, Baccich and De Montluzin, ca. 1910; New Orleans, Louisiana (Western Architect).

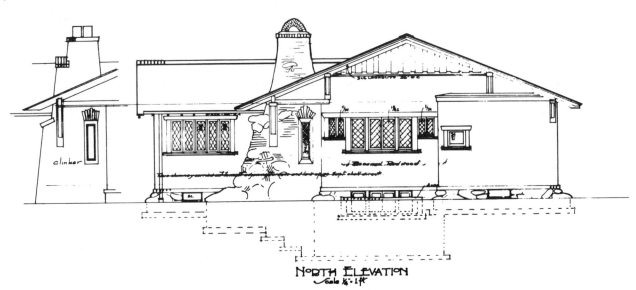

Bungalow #4, St. Francis Court, Sylvanus Marston, 1909; Pasadena. Built on land now occupied by Robinson's Department Store on Colorado Boulevard.

"La Chiquita," Francis T. Underhill, 1904–5; Montecito. Now greatly altered. (David Gebhard)

Unidentified bungalow, Los Angeles area.

The first untaught need of the savage
  The first unskilled work of his hand,
Was a shelter from storm and from ravage—
  The first step by reason o'er-spanned

And down through the ages uncounted
  Since the first dim striving began,
To the marvelous labors surmounted
  That mark the far progress of man.

Though toiling with ploughshare or sabre—
  Wherever his lot has been cast—
At home at the end of his labor,
  Has been his first need and his last.

And ever to mark his advancement,
  To match his refinement of mind,
The home as its added enhancement
  Has been bettered and brightened and fined.

He has learned that in worth, not in seeming,
  The fullness of life must be sought,
And into the home of his dreaming
  This essence of truth has been wrought.

He has found that in fineness and fitness
  Lie beauty and charm, not in show,
As his latest achievement bears witness,
  The beautiful Bungalow.[14]

Notes

1. Clay Lancaster, ''The American Bungalow,'' *Art Bulletin*, 40 (1958): 245–47. See also Reyner Banham's ''Introduction'' to Randell Makinson's *Greene and Greene: Architecture as a Fine Art* (Salt Lake City: Peregrine-Smith, Inc., 1977), p. 23.

2. Anthony King, ''The Bungalow in India: Its Regional and Pre-Industrial Origin,'' *Architectural Association Quarterly*, 5 (1973): 8. As I indicate in the text, I am deeply indebted to Professor King for the information in the first part of this chapter and to his generosity in sharing other aspects of his research with me.

3. Ibid., p. 25.

4. Ibid., p. 8–14.

5. Ibid., p. 16.

6. Ibid., p. 16.

7. R.A. Briggs, ''Bungalows,'' *Studio*, 3 (1894): 20.

8. Clay Lancaster, ''The American Bungalow,'' *Art Bulletin*, 40 (1958): 239.

9. Ibid., p. 239.

10. A.W. Brunner, ed., *Cottages or Hints on Economical Building* (New York: William T. Comstock, 1884), p. 7. The frontispiece and Plate XVII illustrate Brunner's own bungalow.

11. W. Betting and J.J. Vriend, *Bungalows: Deutschland, England, Italien, Holland, Belgien, Danemark* (Darmstadt: H. Muller-Wellbow, 1958); translated from preface and included in Anthony King's, ''The Bungalow: Social Process and Urban Form: The Bungalow as an Indicator of Social Trends,'' *Architectural Association Quarterly*, 5 (1973): 4–5.

12. Lancaster, ''The American Bungalow,'' p. 243.

13. King, ''The Bungalow: Social Process,'' p. 12.

14. Stillwell and Co., *Little Bungalows* (1920), ''Le Dernier Cri.'' The author's name is lost to history.

Another reason for the bungalow's popularity was that it was promoted by a volume of literature almost as prodigious as that which promoted California itself. The sedate eastern publication, *Architectural Record*, rarely mentioned the bungalow. Its editor, Herbert Croly, in a major article (1913) on California architecture, illustrated the work of the tilemaker Ernest Batchelder as well as houses designed by Charles and Henry Greene and Arthur Kelly. But he was more interested in what he thought was the Spanish tradition in California than he was in the bungalow.[1] A few other articles appeared from time to time. The *American Architect* was more generous. Nevertheless, the enthusiasm for the bungalow was to be found largely in the women's magazines, the *Ladies Home Journal* being the most devoted proponent. Gustav Stickley's *Craftsman*, through its Pasadena correspondents, Helen Lukens Gaut and Una Nixon Hopkins, kept in close touch with what was going on in Bungalowland, publishing the work of the Greenes, the Heinemans, Walker and Vawter, Arthur Kelly, Frederick Roehrig, George Clark, and a host of other less notable architects who worked in the bungalow style.[2]

Western-oriented periodicals, especially those for professional builders and architects, took up the cause. The *Western Architect,* although published in Minneapolis, kept its readers well informed on the California phenomenon as well as on similar work in the Midwest. One of the most interesting if least noticed architectural magazines was *Keith's Magazine on Home Building* (1901–26) which published articles about bungalows from the first issue until its demise. *Keith's* major tribute came annually in the April issue, called the "Bungalow Number," which was entirely devoted to analysis of the bungalow's features. The 1915 number, for example, contained such enticing illustrated articles as "A Bachelor's Bungalow," "Building Bun-

Cover of Henry Wilson's Bungalow Magazine.

Concrete bungalow in Puerto Rico. The Article in Keith's *was on the work of Antonin Nechodoma, whose bungalow at San Juan is illustrated here. It apparently dates from about 1915. (Comstock,* Bungalows . . . *p. 88)*

Henry Wilson, the self-styled "Bungalow Man."

Yours for Artistic Homes

Henry L. Wilson

galows Aloft,'' ''Why Bungalows Are So Popular,'' ''The Bungalow'' (an unsigned poem), ''A Suggestion for the Summer Bungalow Living Room,'' ''Building the Bungalow Fire-Proof,'' ''Planting the Bungalow,'' and ''A Bungalow for Father and Mother.''[3] One might think that the subject had been covered, but the next April number included ''Concrete Bungalows in Porto Rico,'' ''Rain on the Roof,'' ''The Bungalow Fireplace'' and many more articles,[4] all highly edifying. In the Far West the *Architect and Engineer of California,*[5] *Arrowhead*[6] (a travel magazine published by the old Salt Lake Route Railroad), and the *Los Angeles Times* strenuously advanced the cause. There was even the *Bungalow Magazine,* completely absorbed with the presentation of the subject and published monthly by the self-styled ''Bungalow Man'' Henry Wilson, first in Los Angeles (1909–10) and later in Seattle (1912–18).

However, the real boosters were the literally dozens of ''bungalow books''[7] published by eager entrepreneurs of the small house. Sold cheaply—often given away—by hopeful contractors and builders, these books were something more (and less) than the ''carpenters' handbooks'' and ''builders' assistants'' that had spread the knowledge of architecture throughout America in the eighteenth and nineteenth centuries. Typically, the bungalow book was composed of photographs or drawings of ''artistic'' bungalows accompanied by simplified floor plans. The reader could get a complete set of drawings for a few dollars; in the early nineteen hundreds sets would cost around $5; by the 1920s, perhaps $25. For a few dollars more the plans could be reversed or adapted to a difficult site. Always the reader was instructed to avoid the temptation to turn over the rudimentary elevation and floor plan to a builder. Disaster was promised in the absence of detailed drawings. But how often was this warning heeded? Thousands of bungalows must have been built directly from the bungalow books' plans, touched up a little by a draftsman.

Bungalow Design No. 5031. Elevation and floor plan from Radford's Bungalows (1908), p. 22. "Blue prints consist of foundation plan; floor plan; front, rear, two side elevations; wall sections and all necessary interior details. Specifications consist of twenty-two pages of typewritten matter." All this for only ten dollars!

Who were the real designers of the small houses in the bungalow books? They will turn up as study continues. They were certainly not always the publishers of the bungalow books, whatever their claims. More often they were boys in the office, and frequently they were well-known architects who had already designed and built the bungalows that were illustrated. For instance, around 1911 Edward E. Sweet, whose motto was "Just a little different," published a bungalow book of elevations, floor plans, and even photographs of interiors as well as exteriors.[8] The quality of the designs varies greatly throughout the book. The frontispiece in color hints at almost Greene-and-Greene sophistication, but most of the offerings inside the book are dreary beyond belief. The unevenness is at least partially explained by a photograph in one of the scrapbooks[9] compiled by the Pasadena architect Alfred Heineman of designs which he created for his brother Arthur's firm. Clearly Sweet's frontispiece bungalow was actually designed by the Heinemans. Indeed, it is good fun for anyone familiar with the work of the Heinemans to go through Sweet's book in order to spot the designs that are "just a little different." All appear to be by the Heinemans.

Rarely are the names of the real designers mentioned in bungalow books, but sometimes under close scrutiny they appear in the shadows. Frequently the name "Ross Montgomery, del." or some variation of that attribution appears in the corner of the most beautiful elevations in Clyde Cheney's *Artistic Bungalows* (1912)[10] and in *Allen Bungalows* (1912).[11] Their refinement suggests that Montgomery, who in the twenties designed the Byzantine-Romanesque Saint Andrew's Catholic Church in Pasadena, was something more than a delineator. But the bungalow entrepreneurs were not generally anxious to share the cult of personality with the designers, who remained anonymous while the entrepreneurs received the publicity.

Bungalow, Arthur S. Heineman (Alfred Heineman, assoc.), ca. 1911. This bungalow appears in color on the cover of Sweet's Bungalows *and also as Plan No. 101 on p. 20. Sweet gives the Heinemans no credit whatsever. (Photograph from Heineman archive, Greene and Greene Library, Gamble House, Pasadena)*

Design from Cheney, Artistic Bungalows, *p. 18. Notice the signature "R.M. DEL." This is for Ross Montgomery.*

The bungalow books were by no means the only examples of the resourcefulness of people who had an eye for financial reward as well as a knowledge of what was artistic. The well-advertised business in prefabricated bungalows also flourished. The California Ready-Cut Bungalow Company, which functioned between 1909 and 1940, promised, "You buy a 'Ready Cut House' and you or your carpenter simply nail it together and 'put it on' the lot—you don't have to wait three to six months for your home to be completed." Every piece of lumber would be cut to fit and carefully loaded on a boxcar with special unloading instructions. The builder could thus save hundreds of dollars in lumber which would normally be wasted in the building of a bungalow. Moreover, the contractor and carpenter would appreciate the fact that what was usually their most unprofitable work was done in a factory. "It is only reasonable," said the advertising department, "to say that studs, joists, rafters, sheathing, flooring, siding, finishing, etc., can be cut on a power-driven saw more cheaply than they can by a hand-workman."[12]

Ready-Cut also would supply at a nominal cost kitchen and bathroom equipment, hardware, lighting fixtures, roofing, paints, and wallboard. The last, it went to great pains to recommend as cheap, fire-resistant, easily applied, soundproof, quickly removed for plumbing and electrical repairs, vermin-proof, and, for a number of other reasons—including the fact that it eliminated the possibility of "hair cracks"—completely satisfactory. In 1919 Ready-Cut would supply lumber, millwork, hardware, roofing, and paint for $672.50. Wallboard would be extra at $43.20. Plumbing fixtures, including tub, stool, wash basin and kitchen sink, laundry tray, and all their fittings and pipes, would be an additional $157.50.[13] Robert Butte, the son of the founder of Pacific Ready-Cut, William Butte, estimates that his father's firm was responsible for

Tract under construction, Los Angeles area.

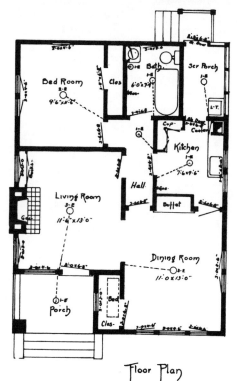

Floor Plan

ESTIMATE ON CONSTRUCTION	
Carpenter Work	$210.00
Mason Work	105.00
Cement Work	89.00
Tin Work	12.00
Plumbing Labor	30.00
Roofing Labor	13.00
Painting Labor	32.00
Electric Wiring	13.50
Bed	30.00
Total	$534.50

California Ready Cut Bungalow Company (bungalow book), p. 3.

roughly 40,000 bungalows in the Los Angeles area alone. With headquarters in Huntington Park, the factory would do everything from laying the foundation to making the final inspection.[14]

Deryck Holdsworth, a geographer at the University of British Columbia, has noted that Canadians merchandised the bungalow in the same way Southern Californians did. Vancouver had at least two 'ready-cut' factories, and the results of their work are still to be seen in the literally acres of tracts, especially in the Kitselano district. Holdsworth's scholarship has turned up another development technique: "us[ing] scale economies in initial land purchase, materials, designs and construction to skillfully manipulate large tracts of land yet still keep the appeal of variety." The Vancouver model, according to Holdsworth, was the Los Angeles Investment Syndicate.[15]

A similar firm was the Southern California Standard Building Investment Company, based in both Los Angeles and San Diego. It published its own bungalow book, of course, but it could promise more than tasteful homes to its readers. In fact, it was directly aimed at the eastern immigrant who was not only looking for a home, but also seeking to establish even more security. Standard would naturally supply plans, but it also would sell houses and lots, farmland, citrus groves, and business property. More than that, "If you have not enough money to build that bungalow you picked out, we can help you with a loan. Is your house insured? Better let us attend to it for you." Did you want to buy an apartment house? "We have good ones listed for sale. We design them and build them—one of our specialties." Standard would even arrange exchanges of eastern property

Street ca. 1925; Kitselano District, Vancouver, British Columbia.

"for something in Sunny California. WE CAN DO IT."[16] One can rarely find a better example of American business savvy.

Like the bungalow itself, the business associated with it was far from being limited to California or to the West Coast. Bungalow books proliferated. Indeed, one of the most widely read, considering the frequency with which it appears in secondhand book shops, was Charles E. White, Jr.'s, *The Bungalow Book*, first published by The Macmillan Company in 1923. White was a member of the "Chicago School,' a group of midwestern architects who regarded Louis Sullivan and Frank Lloyd Wright as the prophets of modern architecture. White's illustrations include a Prairie Style bungalow of his own devising and also one by Frank Lloyd Wright.[17] Nor was merchandising and prefabrication a purely California phenomenon. The Aladdin Company, which had its home office in Bay City, Michigan, specialized in prefabricated bungalows and also larger houses. Aladdin also had distribution and milling centers at Wilmington, North Carolina; Hattiesburg, Mississippi; Portland, Oregon; and Toronto, Ontario (with other mills in Ottawa

and Vancouver). The sales pitch was identical to the California industry's,[18] with bungalows called "The Pomona" and "The Pasadena" and "The Sunshine" apparently selling as well in the rest of the country as in California. Even bungalows advertised outside of California were pictured amidst the lush California rose gardens, and the bungalow books' end papers were illustrated with Kate-Greenaway-influenced pictures of domestic bliss right out of the land of never-ending summer.

"The Pasadena" Aladdin Homes, *p. 43.*

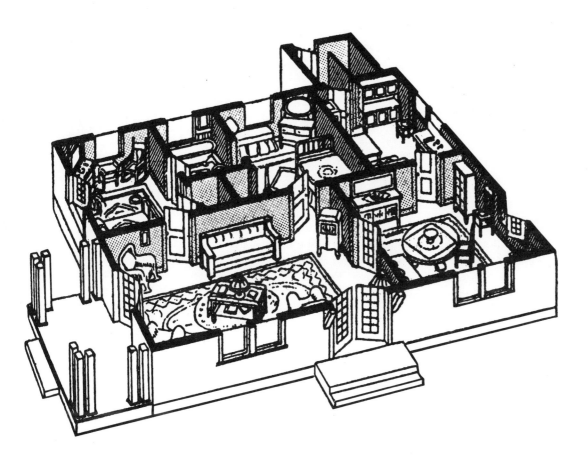

Endpaper, Aladdin Homes. *Notice that "The Pasadena" is in the background.*

Notes

1. Herbert D. Croly, "The Country House in California," *Architectural Record,* 34 (1913): 484–92.

2. The *Craftsman,* published between 1901 and 1916, carried pictures of bungalows in every issue. Strangely, the text accompanying the pictures is not usually very incisive or even informative in comparison to that in other journals and the bungalow books.

3. *Keith's,* 33 (1915): 233–84.

4. Ibid., 35 (1916): 241–88.

5. It contains in a 1917 issue one of the most interesting articles on landscape gardening around a bungalow court in Hollywood: Wilbur David Cook, Jr., "Highbourne Gardens—a Southern California Bungalow Court," *Architect and Engineer,* 50 (1917): 39–45.

6. A cloying but exceptionally informative article on bungalow courts in Pasadena is in "Tours of Pollyann— Pollyann Finds the Ideal Home Life in Pasadena," *Arrowhead* (1917): 21–24.

7. See bibliography section of this book.

8. Edward E. Sweet, *Bungalows* (Los Angeles: Southern California Printing Company, ca. 1911).

9. The Heineman scrapbooks are housed in the Greene and Greene Library at the Gamble House, Pasadena.

10. Clyde Cheney, *Artistic Bungalows* (Los Angeles: Architectural Construction Company, 1912).

11. *Allen Bungalows* (Los Angeles: W. E. Allen Co., 1912). See especially pp. 19–38. Obviously Montgomery was one of the few architects who were strongly influenced by Charles and Henry Greene.

12. California Ready-Cut Bungalow Co. (Los Angeles: ca. 1915), p. 1.

13. Ibid., pp. 1–5.

14. Information kindly provided by Diane Feinberg, who interviewed Robert Butte.

15. Deryck W. Holdsworth, "House and Home in Vancouver," paper given at the British-Canadian Symposium on Historical Geography, "The Settlement of Canada: Origins and Transfer," Kingston, Ontario, September, 1975, p. 9.

16. (Bungalow Book) (Los Angeles and San Diego: The Standard Building Investment Company, ca. 1910), p. 4.

17. Charles E. White, Jr., *The Bungalow Book* (New York: The Macmillan Company, 1923), facing pp. 128 and 84, respectively.

18. *Aladdin Homes* (Bay City, Michigan: The Aladdin Company, 1919), pp. 2–13.

The Plan

How should a bungalow look? Certainly in the first decade of the twentieth century, the answer would almost always have been "brown"! Even from the black-and-white photography of the day, one can see that natural or stained shakes and dark-stained clapboard were almost absolute prerequisites for bungalow building. Occasionally green or gray stains were used, but the basic tone was always earthy. The window sash and the bargeboard along the eaves were often painted white, and the roof, when not shingled, might be an almost white composition material or even vivid red tile. Even so, the early pictures show tracts of bungalows in muted tones, obviously a reflection of the notion that a bungalow should blend with its natural surroundings. The effect, while unified, tends in these old photographs to be ironic: since the bungalows were often on such narrow lots that the only places for trees were in the parkway and the backyard, these bungalow neighborhoods sometimes never had a semblance of their proposed natural setting. Street widening has in many areas eliminated the trees in the parkway, so that today many areas of bungalows have a naked look, made more naked because the buildings themselves are painted a lighter color than originally intended.

Well into the twenties the prevailing style, as often remarked at the time, was a variation on (usually a simplification of) the Swiss chalet, with an Oriental feeling often added by slightly upturned eaves and sometimes a large amount of nonfunctional and very elaborate woodwork around the porch columns. In fact, some bungalow books actually label these eclectic facades "Japo-Swiss." Nineteenth-century architects had experimented with both styles in conjunction with Eastlake and Queen Anne forms. It is sometimes asserted that the Orientalism of the American bungalow shows the broad influence of the Pasadena architects Charles and Henry Greene, who were certainly practitioners of the Japo-Swiss connection. Not a shred of evidence has been produced to show that they

Street, Los Angeles area.

4000 Block, Griffin Ave., Highland Park, Los Angeles.

Bungalow, ca. 1912; Gramercy near Olympic, Los Angeles.

Bungalow, Arthur S. Heineman (Alfred Heineman Assoc.), 1913; Los Feliz district, Los Angeles. (Greene and Greene Library, Gamble House, Pasadena)

Detail of sleeping porch, Gamble House, Greene and Greene, 1908; 4 West-moreland Place, Pasadena.

Mission bungalow, ca. 1910; southeast corner 4th and Hollister, Santa Monica.

introduced the style to California. Like other bungalow designers, Greene and Greene were attracted to both the Swiss and Japanese vogues because of the celebration of wooden architecture they embodied—again an irony in Southern California, an area where dry rot and termites are constant invaders. The Oriental mode was more commonly employed in California than elsewhere in the country—another irony when one considers the problems that Orientals were having in California.

While today's Arts and Crafts enthusiasts might like to go back and stain whole neighborhoods brown, they would have to be careful. From the first, a few white or pink stuccoed Mission Style bungalows were scattered through these neighborhoods. Tudor "black-and-white" work was not uncommon. In the teens and twenties even the Japo-Swiss creations would be painted white and yellow. Concrete bungalows appeared very early, and by the twenties cobblestone or boulder ones were built. And with the popularity in the twenties of period revivals—particularly the Spanish Colonial —the bungalow areas completely lost their earlier sobriety.

Floor plan, Cheney, Artistic Bungalows, *p. 33.*

Styles would change, but the fundamental idea of a convenient little house with style would not. Anyone who has lived in a bungalow realizes its good features. A large living room was made to look larger by being joined by an arch to the dining room. Off the dining room was, of course, the kitchen, sometimes thought to be too small but often recommended for the "little lady's" ability to reach things by taking very few steps. Also connected to the dining room or living room would be a hall, off which one or two bedrooms and a bathroom would open. In the more elaborate bungalows there might be a maid's room off the kitchen. (The maid's room almost disappears in the bungalows of the twenties.) If the house had a third bedroom, there was usually an additional bathroom. Often a screened-in back porch served as a utility area, off which was a door to a basement just large enough for the furnace, in houses where a simple floor heater was not adequate.

Although the advantage of the bungalow was that it was mainly on one floor, the limited space usually necessitated a staircase leading to the attic or more likely a tiny sleeping porch that by the twenties was usually windowed in. The literature, a little embarrassed by this cheating on the original single-story idea, suggested that this space might be used for a study, a game room or a guest room. As the bungalow developed, more and more often the upstairs space was enlarged and used as a sleeping area. In fact, even the early bungalows often have an upstairs bathroom.

A study of floor plans is one of the clearest indicators of the style of living in a period. It is interesting in comparing the bungalow plans to the Victorian plans of the eighteen-nineties to discover what has been changed. The front porch is still there. Obviously the orientation of the bungalow was toward the street, though the idea of privacy inherent in the bungalow gradually turned it to the garden, and later the swimming pool. Almost always the entrance was directly into the living

Bungalow, ca. 1910; 501 Bush Street, Fort Bragg.

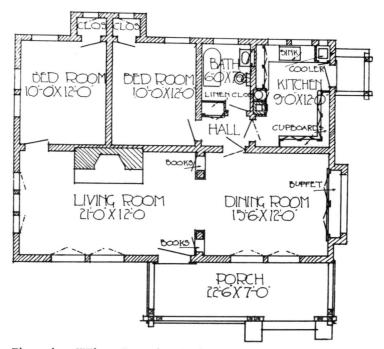

Floor plan, Wilson, Bungalow Book, p. 133.

room. The Victorian entrance hall is gone, as is the Victorian parlor. We notice the centrality of the living room, in the bungalow age actually called a family room. As Robert C. Twombly has noted in his study of Frank Lloyd Wright's open planning, the significance given to the family room (gathering around the fireplace) cannot be overlooked as a symbolic gesture of conserving earlier values in an era of social fragmentation.[1]

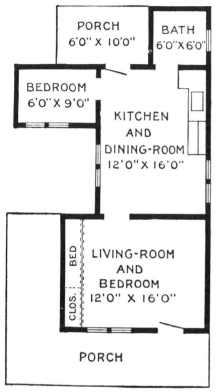

Floor plan, tent bungalow; Los Angeles area.

In the simplest bungalows the dining room was absorbed into the living room, a pull-out table sometimes being the only evidence of the amenities of *haute cuisine*. But usually the dining room retained its individuality—with a few new features! The sideboard (Victorian "buffet") was invariably built-in. Careful reading of the plans often turns up another built-in feature, "the disappearing bed," hidden behind what looks like a closet door. The pantry, an absolute *sine qua non* of the Victorian kitchen, gradually, but only gradually, disappeared. As noted

Barn bungalow, ca. 1910; Los Angeles area. (Los Angeles County Museum of Natural History)

earlier, the maid's quarters also quietly passed away. At the same time kitchens became small and began to be filled with labor-saving devices.

How this change in floor plan occurred deserves some attention. Some writers surmised that since so many bungalows looked like barns, the barn was the source of the style. Many people coming to California had, so these writers fantasized, only enough money to build a barn, another halfway house to the more elaborate home of their dreams. They had fixed up the barn to provide temporary living quarters, which had open spaces adaptable to many uses. Then, if the barn-dwellers had the money, they built their houses. Having experienced the space and the casual quality of their previous dwelling, they were anxious to build it into their new quarters.[2] Thus the bungalow.

However beautifully this explanation corresponds with the back-to-nature syndrome of the age, it should not be taken seriously, as it has been by some modern writers. A better explanation of the peculiar phenomenon called the California bungalow came from romantics who saw it as the modern projection of the Spanish-Mexican hacienda. These writers noted the simple U-shaped, one-story adobe house of the

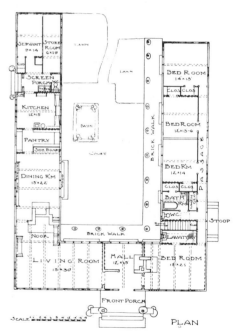

Floor plan, Hollister House, Greene and Greene, 1905; Hollywood, Los Angeles. (Greene and Greene Library, Gamble House, Pasadena)

Opposite: Living room, Batchelder House; Pasadena. (Schenck and Schenck)

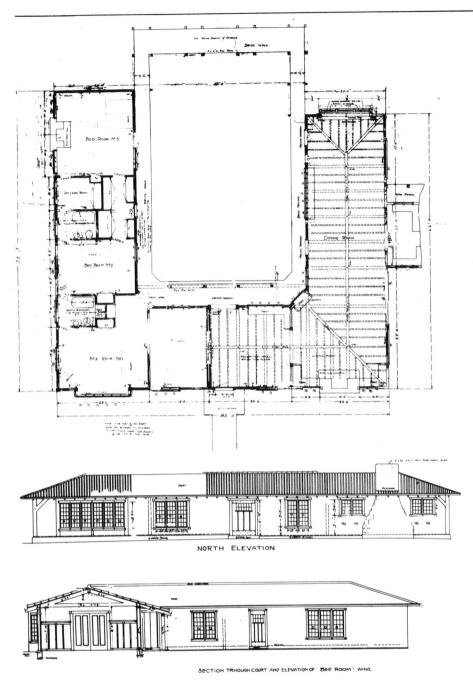

NORTH ELEVATION

SECTION TRHOUGH COURT AND ELEVATION OF "BED ROOM" WING.

Eddy House, Frederick L. Roehrig, 1905. Pasadena

original settlers as a possible model for the convenient but tasteful bungalow.[3] Here again, myth and reality are entangled. While the deepest roots of the bungalow were in the Anglo-Indian tradition, the Hispanic influence, however minimal, should not be discounted. A number of cases exist, for example, in which architects quite consciously copied the U-shaped hacienda plan. However, they made no attempt to imitate the Spanish style of interior decoration except to open the rooms, to be sure by *French* doors, to the interior patio. The Bandini (1903) and Hollister (1904) houses by Charles and Henry Greene were cases in point.[4]

A less publicized example was the Arthur Jerome Eddy house designed in 1905 by the prodigious Frederick Roehrig. Eddy was a successful Chicago lawyer and leader of the Y.M.C.A. movement, who built his house among the orange groves of Pasadena as a refuge from the Windy City. At the southwest corner of Euclid and California the house was, before its recent destruction, an important monument of the Arts and Crafts movement. Eddy, one of the first Americans to write a book about Cubism and Post-Impressionism (1914), brought together in this house Native American pots, Japanese prints, Oriental rugs and hand-crafted objects made in Pasadena. But our interest here is in the fact that, much more directly than the Greenes, he wrote about his house, even giving the impression that he was the designer, an impression picked up and publicized by the *Craftsman* magazine and then by other journals.[5]

From his articles in the *Craftsman* we can certainly believe that Eddy had the inspiration for the U-shaped plan in spite of having to go to Roehrig for architectural expertise. He got his idea from such adobes as the so-called "Ramona's Wedding-House" in Old Town, San Diego. Using what might charitably be called "poetic license," Eddy wrote that his house "simply grew on paper in the course of three or four months, every portion of it being

changed from week to week to meet the requirements of those who were to live in it and the exigencies of the situation, until in the end it simmered down to the plain and simple lines of the native or adobe house, good examples of which still survive and rude examples of which are scattered along the Santa Fe through New Mexico and Arizona. They spring from the soil like sage brush and cactus, they contain germs of life.'' (Actually the blueprints are quite explicit and the house was built exactly to plan.) The bungalow was built on one floor, Eddy wrote, because "In this land of warmth and sunshine and expanse of country, stairs are a nuisance." Obviously relishing the comforts of modern living, Eddy continued, "In the days of the cliff-dwellers and early Pueblos they climbed for protection, but now that life is secure, people may live in comfort on the ground floor, thereby saving endless goings up and down and the incessant trampling of feet overhead or the disturbing sound of muffled voices from below." And the bungalow had to be built around a patio, "for a house in Southern California without a patio is no house at all. It is just a decorated box wherein people swelter. The patio serves three vital purposes; it lets in sunshine in winter; it gathers the breeze in summer; it affords a place for the family to lounge in perfect seclusion or lazily sleep to the soft sound of the splash of water from the fountain." Eddy noted also the advantage that the patio gave for ventilating the house from almost every side in the summer and, with an adopted Californian's sensitivity to the garden, he observed that the warm wall of the house surrounding the patio "prevents the ravages of frost in winter and the tenderest flowers grow like weeds."[6]

Another variation on the patio bungalow was the house which entirely surrounded a patio. The Greenes'

Theodore Irwin House (1906)[7] followed this scheme. But by all odds the most dramatic use of the completely enclosed patio was in the Pitzer House (ca. 1910) designed by Robert H. Orr, who was best known for his churches. A trellis, later glazed, was erected over the patio so that canvas could be rolled across during the hottest part of the day and then rolled back for a view of the Sierra Madre (now called the San Gabriels) in the evening. The patio gained rustic interest because the walls were built of cobblestone, as were the exterior walls. This house, located in Claremont, is in great danger of being destroyed by the completion of the Foothill Freeway.

Many much more modest examples of the bungalow built around a patio were erected. Far more complex plans were developed where a large lot permitted the architect to let his design ramble. But the square or rectangular plan was the most common. Significantly, the patio-house, so urbane in Mexico, Spain, and Peking, was never used as much in Southern California, where residents preferred their houses in the middle of gardens rather than surrounding them.

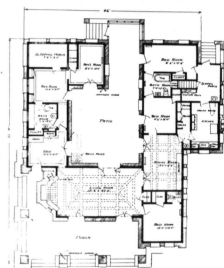

Pitzer House, Robert H. Orr, ca. 1910; southwest corner of Towne and Baseline, Claremont.

Patio, Pitzer House.

There's a jingle in the jungle
'Neath the juniper and pine,
They are mangling the tangle
Of the underbrush and vine,
And my blood is all a-tingle
At the sound of blow on blow,
As I count each single shingle
On my bosky bungalow.

There's a jingle in the jungle,
I am counting every nail
And my mind is bungaloaded,
Bungaloping down a trail;
And I dream of every ingle
Where I angle at my ease,
Naught to set my nerves a-jingle,
I may bungle all I please.

For I oft get bungalonely
In the mingled human drove,
And I long for bungaloafing
In some bungalotus grove,
In a cooling bungalocation
Where no troubling trails intrude,
'Neath some bungalowly rooftree
In east bungalongitude.

Oh, I think with bungaloathing
Of the strangling social swim,
Where they wrangle after bangles
Or for some new-fangled whim;
And I know by bungalogic
That is all my bungalown
That a little bungalotion
Mendeth every mortal moan!

Oh, a man that's bungalonging
For the dingle and the loam
Is a very bungalobster
If he dangles on at home.
Catch the bungalocomotive;
If you cannot face the fee,
Why a bungaloan'll do it—
You can borrow it of me![8]

Notes

1. Robert C. Twombly, ''Saving the Family: Middle Class Atttraction to Wright's Prairie House, 1901–1909,'' *American Quarterly*, 27 (1975): 57–72.
2. The barn as a source of bungalow informality is one of those theories that should be true even if it isn't. Apparently this hypothesis was first stated by an anonymous writer (perhaps Helen Lukens Gaut?) in ''California Barn Dwellings and the Attractive Bungalows Which Have Grown Out of the Idea,'' *Craftsman*, 15 (1909): 598–603. The idea was repeated by many writers as a possibility if not a fact, e.g., M. H. Lazear, ''The Evolution of the Bungalow,'' *House Beautiful*, 26 (1914): 2–5. Strangely even Clay Lancaster apparently finds some credence in it. See his ''The American Bungalow,'' *Art Bulletin*, 40 (1958): 244.
3. The most explicit statement of this hypothesis is in Henry L. Wilson's *The Bungalow Book* (Chicago: published by the author, 1910), p. 3. Even earlier it had been accepted as gospel by Fred T. Hodgson. See his *Practical Bungalows and Cottages for Town and Country* (Chicago: Frederick J. Drake and Company, 1906), especially pp. 6–8. James Tice and Stefanos Polyzoides attribute the U-shaped bungalow court plan to Spanish influence in ''Los Angeles Courts,'' *Casabella* (1976): 17–23.
4. See Randell Makinson, *Greene and Greene: Architecture as a Fine Art* (Salt Lake City and Santa Barbara: Peregrine Smith, Inc., 1977), pp. 70–73 and 88–89. Both houses have been demolished.
5. Arthur Jerome Eddy, ''A California House Modeled on the Simple Lines of the Old Mission Dwelling; Hence Meeting All Requirements of Climate and Environment,'' *Craftsman*, 11 (1906): 211.
6. Ibid. 212–213.
7. See Randell Makinson, *Greene and Greene,* pp. 133–35.
8. Burgess Johnson, ''Bungal-Ode,'' in Henry H. Saylor, *Bungalows* (Philadelphia: John C. Winston Company, 1911), pp. 2–3.

Form and Function

Bungalow, ca. 1910; 745 La Loma, Pasadena.

In this group of low hills and shallow valleys between the Sierra Madre and the sea, the most conspicuous human achievement has been a new form of domestic architecture.

This is the thing that strikes the attention of the traveller; not the orchards and the gardens which are not appreciably different in kind from those of the Riviera and some favoured parts of Italy, but the homes, the number of them, their extraordinary adaptability to the purposes of gracious living. The Angelenos call them bungalows, in respect to the type from which the later form developed, but they deserve a name as distinctive as they have in character become. These little, thin-walled dwellings, all of desert-tinted native woods and stones, are as indigenous to the soil as if they had grown up out of it, as charming in line and the perfection of utility as

some of those wild growths which show a delicate airy fluorescence above ground, but under it have deep, man-shaped, resistant roots. With their low and flat-pitched roofs they present a certain likeness to the aboriginal dwellings which the Franciscans found scattered like wasps' nests among the chapparal along the river—which is only another way of saying that the spirit of the land shapes the art that is produced there.

Mary Austin, *California: The Land of the Sun*[1]

The point of the California bungalow was to get almost everything on one floor. Its exterior charm, when it had any, was at least partly the result of the closeness of that floor to the ground. Good drainage of the soil during even most heavy rains made it possible to put the little house on a very low foundation, thus emphasizing its mainly horizontal lines. Anyone who has seen very similar bungalows in Vancouver, B.C., some of them beautifully designed, realizes that when compared to their California relative, they seem gawky on their often unnecessarily high basements that are usually mostly above ground. The California bungalow seemed to hug the earth. As a writer of bungalow books put it, "the bungalow cannot be built too close to the ground and, indeed,

Bungalow, ca. 1920; 2249 West 35th, Vancouver, British Columbia.

Underhill House, Francis T. Underhill, 1904-5; Montecito. (Marvin Rand)

Opposite: Stewart House, Frank Lloyd Wright, 1909-10; 196 Summit Road, Montecito. (David Gebhard)

the purpose should always be to make the bungalow a harmonious part of the grounds surrounding it. Wide cement porches are frequently laid flat on the surface, so that the indoors and outdoors might be said to join hands."[2]

This is an important point. The author is at once restating the concept of the close relationship of the bungalow to nature and developing a principle of design endorsing the horizontal line as a desirable effect. The significance of this principle in an age of the vertical skyscraper will certainly not be lost on the student of Frank Lloyd Wright or the Prairie School in general. H. Allen Brooks has noted that Henry Saylor, in describing the varieties of bungalows across the nation, referred to the "Chicago-type bungalow."[3] Brooks believes that Saylor's remarks and others like them were important in popularizing the Prairie Style, for it allowed the public "to believe, as they often did, that the Prairie House was not an anomaly but held an approved place in the architectural scene."[4] I would go further and suggest that people were observing a real connection between the Prairie Style and the bungalow. Although I have no documentary proof except that Wright built bungalows, I would surmise that the bungalow was at least one of the sources of the Prairie Style. To push the point even further, I would note that the reason Wright's Prairie Style, redwood-clad Stewart House (1909–10) does not seem to be out of place in the rolling hills of Montecito, California, is that it had its esthetic roots in the California bungalow. Its distinction from its nearby relatives is that it was designed by a genius.

Entering the bungalow, one's immediate impression is that the quarters are cramped, but a little more study shows that the architect or more often "designer" was concerned to make the spaces look as roomy as possible—thus the invariable connection of living room and dining room and also the interest in such devices as the mirror and the inglenook, both devices for manipulating interior spaces.

But it is the design, sometimes taken directly out of *Craftsman* magazine, that unifies all believers in the simple but tasteful house. It was an organization of linear components strongly reflecting the design concepts of the British Arts and Crafts movement—especially those of M. H. Baillie-Scott, Charles Voysey, and Charles Mackintosh. Whatever the style of the exterior, the interior of the living room and dining room in the period before World War I was bound to have a plate rail about eighteen inches from the ceiling. But even more important, in spite of plaster being conspicuous, was a feeling of wood—redwood, Oregon pine, oak, and, in the fancier bungalows, gum and teak. The wood was usually displayed from baseboard to plate rail, the least expensive being simple board-and-batten, the most expensive being vaguely Tudor or as in the Greenes' work, Orientalized. The frieze above the plate rail might be painted in greens or browns, hung in burlap, wallpapered or decorated with stencil-work in stylized flower patterns. Always, even though the bungalow had a floor heater or a furnace in the small basement, there was a fireplace in the living room and sometimes in the dining room as well. The fireplace was given special treatment, in an inglenook or by a rich profusion of boulders or perhaps some Batchelder tiles. The curtains were simple but cheerful. The furniture, though in the bungalow books largely that of Stickley or his adherents, was probably a mixture of Mission Style and family inheritances.

These aspects are the basics of the living room. An enumeration of standard features cannot, however, begin to describe the possibilities of a very high style within this framework. A writer for *Architect and Engineer* (1908) fortunately was very specific in describing what the bungalow people often termed a ''classy'' living room:

The mantel is built of chipped brick; on each side of the fireplace is an inglenook with appropriate cushions. The supporting columns, beams, and

Rarely did the bungalow book author so clearly lift a design directly out of the Craftsman. *Cheney copied this den from the October, 1905 issue and, after adding the gentlemen, inserted it without credit in his* Artistic Bungalows, *p. 33.*

Every piece of oak furniture in this present-day bungalow living room came from Stickley's United Crafts.

furniture are in weathered oak, greenish brown and waxed finish. There are no window shades in this bungalow. Fine fancy net curtains in Arabian color and over these mahogany colored *shikii* silk curtains on separate brass rods and rings take the place of the shade and the consequent roller, allowing the hinged sash to move with perfect freedom.

The Navajo blanket which covers the floor is a proper decoration, as it agrees with the straight lines of the Mission furniture.

The walls in the living room are of rough plaster, painted in oil a warm brown color, and the ceiling between the beams is an orange chrome yellow. To the right may be seen an oil painting on buckskin of an Indian chief, while the baskets and other paraphernalia are reminders that the original inhabitants of the United States are fitted for other accomplishments than the use of the scalping knife and the chase.[5]

Bailey House No. 2, Mead and Requa, 1913; La Jolla. Obviously the Indian motif is stronger here than in the bungalow described in the text.

Inglenook, Volney Craig House,
Louis B. Easton, 1908; Pasadena.
(Brian Thomas)

Cast stone fireplace, 6' x 4½', from
advertisement for the Tay-Mac Co.'s
mantles in Standard Building Invest-
ment Company pamphlet, p. 42.
Notice that the embellishment pictures
the Santa Barbara Mission.

A slightly less dazzling bungalow living room (1908) was that of one Gilbert H. Cunningham of Oakland: *The interior is furnished in brown stained wood in heavy Mission detail, so heavy and unique in form and design as to create an atmosphere of rest and comfort that ordinarily comes from the antique timbering of some old Spanish castle. In carrying out this effect the hall and living-room were paneled with calf hides with the hair left on them, the soft multi-colors blending well with the brown woodwork, leathered wall and arched ceiling.*[6]

Just one more quote, this time from Henry L. Wilson, the self-styled "Bungalow Man" who celebrated the qualities of "the room where the family gathers, and in which the visitor feels at once the warm, homelike hospitality. Everything should suggest comfort and restfulness. The open fireplace and low broad mantel, a cozy nook in the corner, or a broad window seat, are all means to a desired end. . . . Ceiling beams add an air of homely quaintness which never grows tiresome."[7]

Notice the repeated litany of soft earthtones, quaint furniture, and cozy nooks associated with an atmosphere of rest, comfort, warmth, and withdrawal from a world which is somehow too frenzied for anyone constantly to bear. It is also obvious that this scene, especially the Indian artifacts, such as the Navajo rug and portrait of an Indian chief, was intended for the male of the household. The mood of rest and comfort, of ostentatious simplicity, was supposed to calm the male psyche after a hard day at the office or factory. Sometimes writers were quite explicit. One thought that "the beauty and restfulness of little sun parlors caress tired nerves and make new men out of old."[8] In these descriptions "the little lady" is never so much as mentioned.

In the foregoing quotations the word *mission* was used repeatedly—in connection with the woodwork, sometimes with a "Mission finish," that is, stained and lightly varnished, and

Living room in one of the bungalows at the St. Francis Court, Sylvanus Marston, 1909.

Living and Dining rooms, plan No. 303, Sweet's Bungalows, p. 13. Probably designed by the Heinemans.

Mission furniture. The furniture, like the woodwork, had no relationship whatsoever to the Spanish missions, but the word *mission* was apparently applied to both in order to create the mood intended.[9] The foursquare furniture, designed by Gustav Stickley and his imitators in Grand Rapids and even Los Angeles, obviously fit with the right angles of the interior design. Spain, having been recently soundly defeated in war supposedly because of its lassitude, if not decadence, evoked comfort and rest, so why not *mission?*

An interesting fact, pointed out to me by my mother, is that in the Midwest, where she grew up, Stickley furniture was relegated only to the most informal rooms: "We always had our best furniture in the front rooms; the Mission stuff was in the den or sun porch!" A study of old photographs of architecture shows many examples of Stickley furniture in eastern living rooms, but it is important to note how much more of it was found in California interiors, a fact of great importance since the western bungalow, like California itself, was unashamedly looked upon as a retreat, like an eastern lake cottage or mountain cabin, from the "real" world and its over-sophisticated pretention.

One thing the East and West could agree upon was that Mission furniture befitted the billiard room and den, other areas of the male domain. Henry L. Wilson felt that a den, a place of "luxurious rest amid a pile of cushions and surrounded by curios and mementoes which accumulate in every family, each reminiscent of good times gone by,"[10] was almost a necessity in every bungalow. The description of the ambience of the den in the Cunningham bungalow in Oakland is irresistible, if depraved:

Underneath this stair landing Mr. Cunningham has a den or profanity room, so called because no one is allowed to use severe adjectives in any other part of the house. This room has panelled walls and ceilings and all woodwork is fastened with rough, black-headed nails. In this room is a

*Sideboard, Eddy House dining room,
Frederick J. Roehrig, 1905; Pasadena.
(William Current)*

*Dining room, Underhill House,
Francis T. Underhill, 1904–5;
Montecito.*

Dining rooms, kitchen and bathroom in Wilson's Bungalow Book.

writing desk built in and arranged to accommodate several bottles of ink, and whenever his friends call on him, Mr. Cunningham invariably tenders them a glassful of red or amber-colored ink, so they can write down in their memory his invitation to call again and to call often.[11]

The bungalow's dining room was similarly, often threateningly, masculine, though its major feature would be a built-in sideboard, behind whose leaded glass cabinets "the wife" would keep her best china. A chandelier of metal and glass would hang, usually low, over the Stickley dining table. Sometimes this lighting fixture was handsome, but often it was aggressively hideous. Even in the latter case it was designed in an attempt to establish a unified whole—a poor man's version of Frank Lloyd Wright's "organic" dining room at the Robie House or the Greenes' at the Gamble House.

Although the dining room usually continued the sombreness of the living room, it could also be extraordinarily rich. In the Cunningham bungalow, for example, "the dining . . . room has panelling of gold bronze Spanish leather, while the ceiling which slopes upward from all sides to the center, is covered with Japanese burlap." And the masculine esthetic is maintained in the staircase landing, where "there are some large windows which have been filled with art glass in a design representing the bottom of the sea and in which are great red and speckled fish floating lazily about."[12] Enough to chase the worries from the most harrassed husband. The fish might even remind him of his cabin in the mountains or a day off the coast of Catalina!

If the living and dining rooms of the bungalow were the seat of male chauvinism, the bedrooms, kitchen, and bathrooms were the province of women. I mean this as no cheap artistic maneuver. The bedrooms, while often paneled, were usually painted white or a very light color. Where the dark living room might be cheered by a fire behind the andirons and a few

spots of light created by lamps, the bedrooms were usually bathed in light from banks of windows. It was here that wallpapers might be used—by 1915 little blue and white stripes and "nosegays of Colonial days."[13]

Another strange fact (the period is full of ambivalence) is that the kitchen, the woman's domain, was, besides the bathroom, the most "modern" part of the house as far as convenience and utility were concerned. While the male escaped from the daytime machine to his evening hideaway, his wife was busying herself with so many mechanical gadgets that they must often have gotten in the way. In an age which believed that a woman's place was in the home, it is curious that it should have made her sanctum sanctorum, the kitchen, into a factory. But the curious is easily explained: In a sense she was doing the most important work, keeping the family together in an age which believed that the family was threatened. Why should she not have every convenience so that she could accomplish her healing mission? As Henry L. Wilson put it, "Saving of steps in the kitchen means conservation of energy and health, and consequently promotes the general welfare of the family."[14]

Charles E. White, writing in 1923, when the bungalow had reached full maturity, put at the top of his list of important kitchen machinery an "electric kitchen cabinet." This device would look like the conventional counter with cabinets above, but would contain an electrically driven revolving shaft to which all the food-preparing devices might be attached. The kitchen, he continued, should have every other electrical device possible, including a range, portable oven, toaster, percolator, hot plates, chafing dishes and a dishwarmer. "Your kitchen is your factory," he wrote.[16] The principle of electric refrigeration, although known, had not yet been sold very widely. Possibly that is the reason

for White's omission of it. But, significantly, while he was thinking about electrical labor-saving devices in the kitchen, he went on to suggest electrical phonographs, furnaces, "hot water heating faucets," vacuum cleaners, and washers—all, except the phonograph and furnace, intended to liberate women from drudgery.[17]

The plan of the bungalow kitchen also deserves comment. Usually it was small and was sometimes criticized for its lack of space, possibly (though I have no proof of this) because it was not commodious enough to allow the entire family to congregate there, as it had in the Victorian kitchen. But what the kitchen lost in familial integration, it gained in practicality for the individual. All the gadgets and all the built-ins were right at hand—bread boards, flour and sugar bins, cupboards, and ironing boards. Often the kitchen contained a breakfast nook with built-in table and seats.

The bathroom was nearly perfected in machinery, if not in style, in the nineteenth century and should only be mentioned because it was the model of "form follows function." Another nineteenth-century invention was the solar water heater, sometimes used in the bungalow. As I observed long ago, the raison d'etre of the bungalow was not only its charm, but also its utility. C. E. Schemerhorn wrote in 1924, "Fittings for a bungalow should be condensed as the equipment of a yacht." He then summarized the clever economies: "the built-in buffet, crystal and china closets for the dining room, bookcases, medicine closets, folding washstands, etc. Other space-savers consist of disappearing beds, double-purpose revolving furniture, collapsing-rod clothes hangers for closets, and shoe-racks."[18]

The "ultimate bungalow," I fear, was not built in Los Angeles but in Chicago. There a Mr. Adam Int-Hout constructed (ca. 1917) a "folding bungalow" which pressed efficiency to its ultimate conclusion. Writing for the *Architectural Record*, Robert H. Moulton described the ingenious if unnerving Int-Hout tour-de-force. In

physical appearance the bungalow seemed conventional, if quite small. It was twenty-six feet square, but it had a "living-porch" in front that made it look bigger. Nevertheless, you had to go inside to experience its wonders, where, Moulton wrote, "more of the essentials of fine living are compressed into a smaller space than in any similar structure ever built."[19]

The best way to discover the house's secrets was to be invited to dinner. As you were cordially received in the living room, you noticed the bookshelves built into the staircase and, if you looked very carefully, could see that the furnace, carefully designed to send heat all over the house, was hidden behind a grill of vertical boards very much like (Moulton does not say this) the interior architectural device employed for staircases by C. A. Voysey and Irving Gill. But hard as you might try, you could not immediately discover the dining room. Oblivious to your confusion, the hostess left the living room to go to the kitchen "for no maids upset the scheme of harmonious living that this family is working out."[20]

You are relieved when
Mrs. Int-Hout appears and hooks the kitchen door back and you immediately begin to rub your eyes. Heavens! is the wall really moving? Your hostess stands there calmly with her hand on the door casement, seeming barely to touch it, and yet the whole piece of wall is turning round into the kitchen. You know this because the pictures are going into the kitchen as fast as they can, while with equal celerity a small hanging china cabinet comes into view on what was the kitchen side of the partition. Nor is this all, for along with the china cabinet comes a dining room table, in all the splendor of china and glass and snowy napery and tempting viands. The table appears to be fast to the wall until Mrs. Int-Hout gives it a touch with her hand, whereupon it takes its position exactly in the centre of that half of the living room.[21]

Entrance hall, Volney Craig House, Louis B. Easton, 1908. (Brian Thomas)

Observing that "a half mile at least of needless walking has been avoided by setting the table in the kitchen where everything is close at hand," Moulton was equally appreciative of the fact that after dinner the table was swung around again to a place near the kitchen sink where the dishes were to be washed.[22] Almost everything had been thought of.

Needless to say, the quest for functionalism was rarely pursued this far, but as an exaggerated case, the description of the Int-Hout house underlines the fact that the bungalow was not entirely an escape into a picturesque past, but was at least intended to be progressive. It was successful enough to raise critics who laughed at its modern economies:

This is the song of the bungalow,
With a buffet built in the wall
And a disappearing bed beneath
That won't disappear at all;
A song of the folding Morris chair
That never will fold until
You plant your weary carcass there
And sprawl in a sudden spill;
The song of the dinky writing desk
That hangs from a sliding door
Which sends you kiting galley west
Until you write no more;
The song of the pretty porcelain tub,
With a flour bin below,
And a leak that springs on the bread-to-be
While on the floor runs liquid dough;
A song of the handy kitchenette
That is almost two feet square
And all undefiled by the sordid job
Of cooking dinner there;
A song of the lidded window seat,
Where no one could ever sit,
And of plate racks that come crashing down,
And of shelves no books would fit;
A song of pantry and bureau drawers
That will never go in or out—
Oh, a song for all "built-in features"
That we read so much about.

Kind friend, if you capture a bungalow,
Keep it, and your soul, unmarred,
By taking a kit and a sleeping bag
And living right out in the yard.[23]

Notes

1. Mary Austin, *California: The Land of the Sun* (London: Adam and Charles Black, 1914), pp. 29–30.

2. *Radford's Artistic Bungalows* (Chicago: The Radford Architectural Company, 1908), p. 3.

3. H. Allen Brooks, *The Prairie School: Frank Lloyd Wright and his Contemporaries* (Toronto and Buffalo: University of Toronto Press, 1972), p. 20.

4. Ibid., p. 21.

5. "Some California Bungalow and Residence Interiors," *Architect and Engineer of California*, 14 (1908): 45.

6. A. W. Smith, "An Attractive Oakland Bungalow," *Architect and Engineer of California*, 14 (1908): 45.

7. Henry L. Wilson, *The Bungalow Book* (Chicago: published by the author, 1910), p.4.

8. *Radford's Artistic Bungalows*, p. 3.

9. Gustav Stickley, whose designs were apparently the inspiration for this Mission furniture, himself denied that it had any connection with California missions in his "How Mission Furniture Was Named," *Craftsman*, 16 (1909): 225. It must be said that his disavowal of California connections is not completely convincing since the straightforward furniture (possibly designed by Bernard Maybeck) for A. Page Brown's Swedenborgian Church (1894) in San Francisco clearly antedates Stickley's "Craftsman" style. The origin of this style should be clarified.

10. Wilson, *The Bungalow Book*, p. 4.

11. A. W. Smith, "An Attractive Oakland Bungalow," *Architect and Engineer of California*, 14 (1908): 45.

12. Ibid.

13. H. P. Keith, "What to Put In a Bungalow," *Keith's*, 33 (1915): 239.

14. Wilson, *The Bungalow Book*, p. 4.

15. Charles E. White, *The Bungalow Book*, p. 155.

16. Ibid., p. 154.

17. Ibid., p. 160.

18. C. E. Schemerhorn, "Planning the Bungalow" in William Phillips Comstock, *Bungalows, Camps and Mountain Houses* (New York: The William T. Comstock Co., 1908), p. 19.

19. Robert H. Moulton, "A Folding Bungalow," *Architectural Record*, 44 (1918): 93.

20. Ibid.

21. Ibid.

22. Ibid., p. 94.

23. "Ballad of the Bungalow," *Architect and Engineer*, 36 (1914): 111.

Batchelder Tile, ca. 1925. Such tiles were used as advertising gimmicks.

Implications and Innovations

An extraordinary bungalow at 853 Walker Street in Oakland.

California transforms a dandy into a natural man. Both photographs are portraits of George Harris, the first ca. 1890, the second 1933.

It is sometimes said that the mild California climate is debilitating to mental faculties. This supposedly accounts for the madness associated with Hollywood and sometimes even the Bay Area. The more favorable view is that the perpetual sunshine contributes to a casual style of living, much slower paced than that of New York City or Indianapolis. The positive and the negative attitudes toward the influence of the climate are part of the myth of California developed mainly in the East and in a sense exploited by Californians, such as Charles Fletcher Lummis who graduated from Harvard and then went native, collecting Indian pots and entertaining the artistic elite in his rustic salon on the banks of the Arroyo Seco.[1]

Like all myths, "casual California living" has elements of reality, as both admirers and scoffers have noticed. Moreover, the myth has given identity to large numbers of Californians. The exaggerated cases, like Lummis, stand out. Another, George Harris, deserted the publishing business in New York and, when he reached California, exchanged his Prince Albert for knickers and a vest and began making some of the most extraordinarily rustic garden furniture ever conceived of.[2] Still another "natural man" more closely identified with the bungalow, was Carl Curtis, a graduate in electrical engineering of Case Polytechnic Institute in Cleveland. After getting his degree, Curtis came to Los Angeles to find a job. Immediately he succumbed to the image and decided to raise chickens (later dogs) in what is now Altadena. So far as his family knows, he never practiced electrical engineering again.

But this is not to say that Curtis forgot his education. He had an educated eye for style. Family tradition has it that one day when he was walking on Marengo in Pasadena, he passed a bungalow whose sophisticated rusticity attracted him. He asked another pedestrian who the owner might be. The fellow said that he was the owner

*Curtis Ranch house, Louis B. Easton,
1906. General view, living room and
hall looking toward dining room.*

and designer, Louis B. Easton, a retired manual arts instructor from Illinois. Curtis and Easton (whose wife, Honor, incidentally, was the sister of Elbert Hubbard, the ''Sage of East Aurora,'' N.Y. and founder of the Roycroft Arts and Crafts Colony) developed a lasting friendship which resulted in Easton's designing Curtis's bungalow and servants' quarters on what is now Lincoln Avenue in Altadena. *Design* is perhaps not the right word—the story is that the two intuitively developed the work as they went along.[3] At any rate, at first under Easton's direction and then later on his own, Curtis set about constructing all the furniture in the house, some of which can be seen clearly in old photographs, which also show Navajo rugs and southwestern Indian baskets, a diptych of John Muir and John Burroughs, a good library, and, of course, a football pennant from Case.

No question that the California mystique was intimidating but certainly not debilitating. A great many immigrants came from the East to regain health, if not youth; Easton, for instance, believed he had tuberculosis —but it is important to note that even sickness turned the architect to innovation. I have already observed that the sleeping porch was an almost *sine qua non* of bungalow architecture. Open or screened-in, it provided not only a good sleeping room in the summer, but sometimes a healthy bedroom the year 'round. Randell Makinson, the biographer of the architects Greene and Greene, discovered in his research on the famous Gamble House that one of the upstairs rooms labeled ''boys' room'' never had any beds in it, but the house did have a sleeping porch where the boys developed robust physiques.[4]

The apotheosis of the sleeping porch: The Gamble House, Greene and Greene, 1908; 4 Westmoreland Place, Pasadena. (Greene and Greene Library, Gamble House)

But the sleeping porch was a relatively expensive innovation in bungalow design. A much more radical and infinitely cheaper health-oriented addition was the "tent bungalow." Usually, this was a small house, often at the rear of a larger bungalow. Because it was usually only one small room, it could be framed simply so that at least one side and ideally all four could be open to the elements. Canvas curtains could be dropped to keep out infrequent high winds, cold, and rain. Otherwise, the inhabitants were at home with nature. Naturally, since these were simple structures, few of them remain except in old photographs. H. V. von

Holst, a Chicago architect and friend of Frank Lloyd Wright, was intrigued by the tent bungalows and illustrated a number of examples in his *Modern American Homes* (1915), where they share pages with the work of high-art architects such as Greene and Greene, Walter Burley Griffin, and Wright.[5] Henry Saylor also illustrated several tent bungalows in his *Bungalows* (1911), a classic in the bungalow literature.[6]

Also related to the cult of health was the "bungalow court" idea. Its roots go back to groupings of cottages built usually in religious campgrounds from Martha's Vineyard to Chautauqua to Winona Lake in Indiana and beyond. One of the first, if not the first, true

Interior, tent bungalow, Von Holst, Modern American Homes, *Plate 75.*

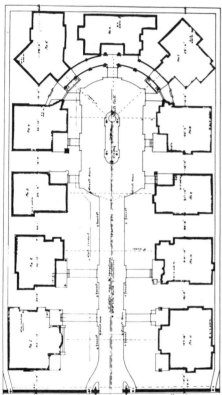

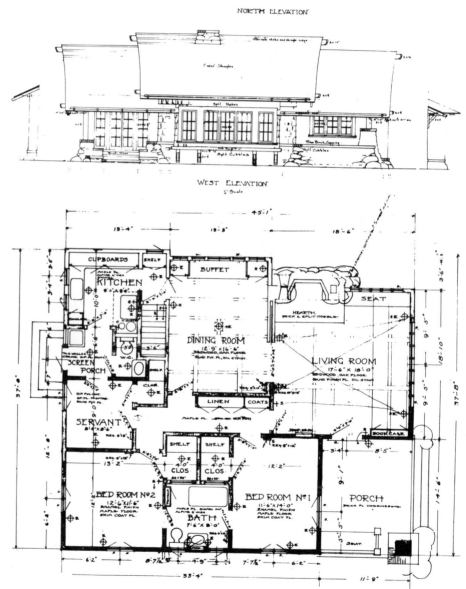

NORTH ELEVATION

WEST ELEVATION

St. Francis Court, Sylvanus Marston, 1909; Pasadena. Probably the first bungalow court in America. When Robinson's Department Store was built at this site, some of these bungalows were moved, five of them to the intersection of Cornell and Catalina in Pasadena. The elevation pictures bungalow No. 11; the floor plan is that of No. 4.

bungalow courts which went by the name was designed by Sylvanus Marston in Pasadena. The permit book at the Pasadena City Hall registers May 14, 1909, as the date Marston presented his plans to the city. The project was a grouping of eleven bungalows around a central court. The quality of the landscaping as well as the architecture suggests that this court was designed to attract the rich who were tired of midwestern ice and snow and also tired of Pasadena's thriving resort hotels, such as the Maryland, the Green, the Raymond, and the Huntington. In fact, several of the bungalows included servants' rooms to ensure that the vacation would be in the style to which the renter was accustomed. Also, the interiors were well designed and outfitted with Stickley furniture, oriental rugs, and real oil paintings, as well as hangings, silver, and kitchen utensils. And the setting on Colorado Street (now Boulevard) was utterly magnificent. According to Henry Saylor, whose *Bungalows* illustrated the court and two interiors, the builders, the Frank G. Hogan Company, had no trouble in renting these bungalows for $1,000 to $1,500 a year or $900 to $1,200 during the winter months.[7]

St. Francis Court, No. 4 as designed and No. 4 as built.

Writing for the *Architectural Record* in 1919, Peter B. Wight gave the credit for the bungalow court idea to Arthur S. Heineman. He compounded his error by noting that the source of the idea was a tuberculosis sanatorium which Heineman had designed in Marion, Ohio, in 1910.[8] Heineman, who had obviously picked up on Marston's idea, actually had his own Los Robles Court under construction by this time.

Although not the originator, Heineman and his younger brother Alfred certainly capitalized on the idea of bungalow courts, usually planning them for people with somewhat lower incomes than Marston's court serviced.

Bowen Court, Arthur S. Heineman (Alfred Heineman, assoc.), 1912; 539 East Villa, Pasadena. (Greene and Greene Library, Gamble House, Pasadena)

Overleaf; Los Robles Court, Arthur S. Heineman (Alfred Heineman, assoc.), 1910; this court was built where the Pasadena Hilton now stands. (Greene and Greene Library, Gamble House, Pasadena)

Alexandria Court, Arthur S. Heineman (Alfred Heineman, assoc.), 1914. This adjoined the Los Robles Court. (Greene and Greene Library, Gamble House, Pasadena)

Lewis Court, Irving Gill, 1910; Mt. Trail and Allegria Streets, Sierra Madre.

The Los Robles Court, now demolished, was a huge success—so much so that they built the Alexandria Court on a slightly larger lot next door in 1914. The Alexandria featured a central heating plant for all the cottages in addition to the common laundry and drying yard that were also provided in the Los Robles Court. Heineman's Bowen Court (1911), which still exists in almost mint condition on Villa Street, was the largest of his Pasadena courts with twenty-three bungalows set on an L-shaped lot. At its center was a rustic clubhouse, with a playroom for the children on the first floor and a sewing room for the ladies on the second.[9]

The bungalow court idea received a few negative reivews. No less an authority than Charles Sumner Greene wrote, "The bungalow court idea is to be regretted. Born of the ever-persistent speculator, it not only has the tendency to increase the cost of the land, but it never admits of home building."[10] Of the Bowen Court, the arch-individualist Greene remarked, "In this bungalow court, the speculator and designer seem to have been the

same mind or the same person. It would seem to have no other reason for being than that of making money for the investor. The style and design of each unit is uniform, making for the monotony and dreariness of a factory district. Added to this, the buildings are hopelessly crowded." And he ended with unwanted didacticism: "This is a good example of what not to do."[11]

Looking at the Bowen Court today, it is very difficult to believe that Greene actually visited it. Needless to say, other observers of bungalow courts were considerably more sympathetic to them. An enthusiastic, not to say ecstatic, admirer was the author of an article for *Arrowhead*. Writing under the well-deserved pseudonym "Polly-ann," this booster claimed to have been asked by "Isabel," a friend in Chicago, to find her a place to stay while making a winter visit to Pasadena. "I jumped into my 'Olds' and in a few minutes was rolling along the Huntington Drive with the beautiful

Sierra Madres towering above and my mind filled with a hope, that right in their shadows, I might find something that would please my Isabel." Sure enough, she found the Heinemans' Alexandria Court, whose bungalows "are only a step away from Colorado Street and yet so quietly situated that they convey the idea of being way off by themselves. I do not know how the architect and landscape designer combined to develop the effect, yet it is there. Once the borders of the delightful courts are passed, one feels as if they were in another land with beautiful flowers, green lawns, and beautiful little homes to fill the picture and every nook and crannie bathed in golden sunlight save where the fronds of splendid palms cast their shadows." Pollyann went on to describe the neighboring Los Robles Court, whose redwood shakes harmonized with the trees and flowers. Returning to the bungalow she had chosen, she described the "hospitable living room with a pretty mantle and fireplace" supplementing the heating and hot water coming from a central source and the white-painted kitchen with its

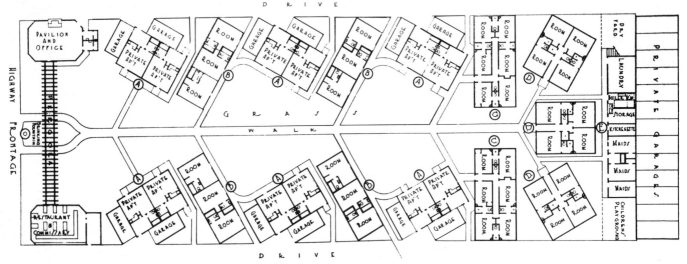

Milestone Mo-tel, Arthur S. Heineman (Alfred Heineman, assoc.), 1924–25; 2223 Monterey Street, San Luis Obispo. Elevation and plan. (Greene and Greene Library, Gamble House, Pasadena)

breakfast nook: ''Not a thing is lacking. All one needs is to bring along their trunk, move in, and telephone for the grocer.''[12]

Historians quite naturally tend to illustrate their writing with the best they can find of the genre, thus suggesting to the reader an amount of work of high quality which simply did not exist. Every one of the literally thousands of bungalow courts in Southern California cannot come up to the high standards of the Heinemans and Marston. But it is surprising how many come off extremely well. They may have been a speculator's dream, but they also performed a service. While designed at first for the vacationing easterner and midwesterner, the courts could be and were adapted to the use of people with moderate or lower incomes; thus, the bungalow courts extended at least a touch of "casual California living" even to the poor. For the social historian not enslaved to high art, the very simple bungalow courts which still function in Pasadena, Hollywood, San Diego, Santa Ana, Seattle, and Vancouver are at least as interesting as the work of the masters.

Stylistically, the "Japo-Swiss" vogue predominated in the bungalow court in the period before World War I. Occasionally the developer used the Mission Revival style with a bell comprising the lighting fixture in the center of the courtyard. After the war the period styles were used, the Spanish Colonial and Islamic revivals being perhaps the most popular. But there were Tudor, Norman, Dutch Colonial, and later Art-Deco and Moderne courts, the most hilarious style being the Egyptian Revival set off by the discovery of King Tut's tomb. Important was the tendency to try to unify these assemblages not only with a stylistic theme, but also a design focus —some imposing feature such as an entry gate or a tower in the rear. These courts took on the character of story-book communities which were just as enjoyable to outside connoisseurs as to the occupants.

Surely by this time the reader has already suspected an extension of the bungalow court idea—the motel. This ought to be true, and is! The name "Mō-Tel" was registered with the Library of Congress, December 24, 1925, by Arthur S. Heineman. In fact, his brother Alfred, the designing member of the firm since 1909, had earlier prepared Spanish-Colonial-Revival drawings for the first motel in America, the "Milestone Mō-Tel," which opened at San Luis Obispo on December 12, 1925. By a stroke of fortune, this motel still operates—altered to be sure—beside Highway 101. Originally, the Milestone was constructed like Heineman's bungalow courts, with garages added, of course.[13]

Pueblo Revival Court, ca. 1917; 3933-45 Hamilton, San Diego.

Tudor Revival Court, ca. 1925; Kitselano District, Vancouver, British Columbia.

Egyptian Revival Court, possibly J.M. Close, ca. 1925; 1428 South Bonnie Brae, Los Angeles. (David Gebhard)

One of the most interesting ways the bungalow identified with the California life style was through its garden. The landscape architect, Wilbur David Cook, Jr., writing about his work on a large bungalow court, "Highbourne Gardens" in Hollywood, noticed that "there is a growing demand for individual houses in park-like surroundings, where one can step from the house into a garden of evergreen beauty, with the feeling that it is yours to enjoy without the responsibility of its upkeep."[14] Few pictures of these bungalow gardens remain, and even fewer actual bungalow gardens, the design by Kate Sessions for the Easton-Mertz house (1906–7) in La Jolla being the best preserved that I know of. But Eugene Murmann's *California Gardens* (1914) is testimony to Herbert Croly's observation that Californians, drenched with sunshine, were especially conscious of their gardens.[15] In a series of designs, only a few of which are reproduced here, Murmann suggested that every bungalow dweller had a choice from formal to English landscape to oriental. Probably few of these designs were ever carried out, but the idea of the extension of the bungalow into a garden is important for the understanding of the bungalow mystique. Landscape architecture, usually the province of the few, was the property of the many.

Easton-Mertz House, Emmor Brooke Weaver, 1907; 1525 Torrey Pines Road, La Jolla. Garden designed by Kate Sessions.

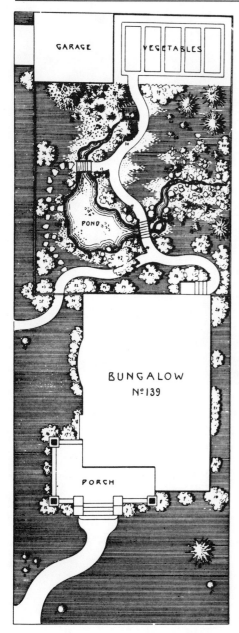

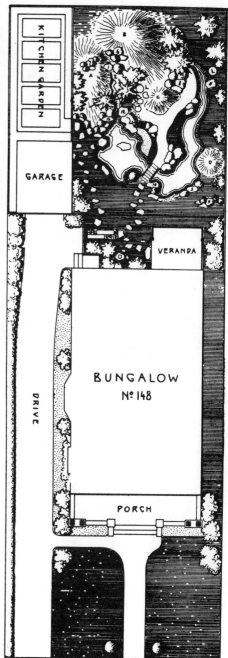

Japanses hill garden, formal garden and rock and water garden from Murmann, California Gardens, pp. 77, 69 and 93.

Garden, St. Francis Court, from
Murmann, California Gardens p. 43.

Central fountain and garden, St.
Francis Court.

SIDE ELEVATION

PLAN
¼" Scale

Garden, Los Angeles area. (Los Angeles County Museum of Natural History)

Polytechnic School, Myron Hunt and Elmer Grey, 1907; 1030 East California at Wilson. (Polytechnic School)

Another fascinating projection of the bungalow idea was the bungalow school, in a sense a spin-off from the tent bungalow. Possibly the first, certainly one of the earliest, of these schools was Pasadena's Polytechnic School, designed in 1907 by Myron Hunt and Elmer Grey. Although the school has been greatly altered and enlarged over the years, one can still see what was intended. The original one-story building was U-shaped with the eaves extending out to form a porch around the inside of the U. The walls of the classrooms could be rolled back so that the children could enjoy the fresh air on good days and have classes outside when possible. In 1911 the architect Norman F. Marsh designed another bungalow school, Nordhoff High School in Ojai, so that "every window will extend to the floor and will swing open their [*sic*] entire length. The pupils will in ordinary weather practically work out of doors."[16] Needless to say, many of the best modern California architects have developed this idea in designing school buildings.

Kindergarten, Roosevelt School, Arthur S. Heineman (Alfred Heineman, assoc.), 1916.

First Congregational Church, 1912; Glendale. (First Congregational Church)

One last offspring of the bungalow phenomenon—the bungalow church. Not many of these were built; few remain, and most of these have been remodeled beyond recognition as bungalows. But, considering again the conception of the bungalow as a celebration of family life which seemed in danger at the turn of the century, the bungalow church was an inevitable development. If the family seemed threatened by the industrial order, the church was in even greater trouble. The late nineteenth century had seen attendance, particularly that of the working classes, dwindling and ministers' salaries, always a barometer of religious enthusiasm, plummeting. The outlook was no brighter in the early twentieth century.

The answer, at least the Protestant answer, was the "social gospel," an interpretation of Christ's message for an industrial society.[17] The social gospel put Christianity solidly on the side of the lower-middle class. Like the political "Progressivism" of the times, the social gospel, whatever its apparent attraction to radicalism, even Marxism, was conservative, longing for a better day before men were alienated from their work—and their families.

Symbolically and functionally, the bungalow church fit into this people-oriented mood of the times. Elsie A. Waggoner, in an article (1914) for the *Los Angeles Times,* wrote of "The Bungalow Church, a Southland Novelty: New Social Spirit." Referring to nineteenth-century church building, she spoke of the absurdity of building Norman and Gothic structures, especially when they had to be done in shingles not used in medieval ecclesiastical building. A new architecture was needed, she believed, to reflect a change in thought about the relationship between the church and the people. Churches were trying to get in touch with everyday life and showing respect for their neighbors as well as their parishioners. What could be more fitting in an area of bungalows than to have a bungalow church, a kind of clubhouse for the neighborhood? Other places in America, she noted, anticipating the huge institutional churches of the twenties, had built substantial buildings, "but Southern California, always original, and especially so in matters architectural, has solved the problem of church planning in an altogether unique way, and the bungalow church is the result." Although carefully planned, the churches she illustrated were informal both in exterior detail and interior appointment, informality being "the keynote of the everyday church." The auditorium of one church costing between $1,000 and $2,000 had a roomy pulpit "big enough for a volunteer choir." At each end of the building were rooms for conventional purposes, but these could be opened by pushing back sliding doors and thus extending the space.

Another church in Hollywood had a porch at the side with wide windows opening to it. "The glass is uncur-

Overleaf: First Christian Church, ca. 1910; Santa Ana. A rather exaggerated example of the bungalow church.

tained save by the fronds of palms and the tassel-like leaves of pepper trees, through which one has glimpses of the soft blue hills, and one who cannot worship in such a room has no spirit of worship in him, whatever his creed or lack of creed.'' Still another bungalow church in the Wilshire district had windows curtained with ''Russian crash edged with lace, a home touch.'' Instead of pews it had chairs which might be moved so as to turn to a stage which was the focus of social functions. In all of these churches there was a fireplace in some part of the sanctuary to underline the ''home touch.'' Indeed Waggoner remarked that because of its homelike atmosphere the Wilshire church survived a long period without a pastor and actually grew in membership.[18]

Now it is quite likely that the attribution of salvation to bungalow simplicity was in part a rationalization of necessity. The twenties were to see most of these churches pulled down to make way for large institutional churches in the various period styles. Like some bungalows, many bungalow churches were merely temporary quarters until more ostentatious edifices could be built. But the timing of the homey church in the period before World War I is significant. It further emphasizes Twombly's point that among the great concerns of the Progressives was the renewal of old values identified with the hearth and home, sorely endangered by material progress. In the midst of a society that was becoming increasingly organized in industrial patterns, it was important for the conservative forces to counter the major social tendencies of the times with a plea for informality, neighborliness, the sanctity of the family. The bungalow church, like the bungalow school so beautifully attuned to John Dewey's concepts of progressive education, performed this service.

Notes

1. See Dudley Gordon, *Charles F. Lummis: Crusader in Corduroy*, (Los Angeles: Cultural Assets Press, 1972).

2. See Esther McCoy, ''George Harris'' in *California Design: 1910*, ed. Timothy J. Andersen, Eudorah M. Moore and Robert W. Winter (Los Angeles: Andersen, Ritchie and Simon, 1974), pp. 110–11; also my essay, ''The Arroyo Culture'' in the same publication, pp. 14–16.

3. See [Timothy Andersen], ''Louis B. Easton'' in *California Design: 1910*, pp. 22–23.

4. Information supplied by Randell Makinson, whose book, *Greene and Greene: Architecture as a Fine Art* (Salt Lake City: Peregrine-Smith, 1977), is the standard work on the Greenes.

5. H. V. von Holst, *Modern American Homes* (Chicago: American Technical Society, 1915), plates 69 and 75.

6. Henry H. Saylor, *Bungalows* (Philadelphia: The John C. Winston Company, 1911), pp. 33, 35, and 38. Several of these bungalows were moved to a site at and near the northwest corner of Wilson and Arden. They were discovered by William Cross of the Pasadena Cultural Heritage Program.

7. Ibid., p. 25. John Chase gave me the suggestion of the origin of the court in the summer camp meeting. William Cross unearthed the date of the Marston court. Laura Chase, the leading authority on the bungalow court, has kindly shared her research with me. She finds yet another source—the ''house court'' or ''cholo court,'' the Los Angeles version of the tenement. See Bessie Stoddard, ''Courts of Sonoratown'' *Charities* [Los Angeles], 15 (December 2, 1905): 295–98.

8. Peter B. Wight, ''Bungalow Courts in California,'' *Architectural Record*, 29 (1919): 16.

9. All of this material is documented in the scrapbooks that Alfred Heineman compiled and presented to the Greene and Greene Library at the Gamble House, Pasadena, shortly before his death.

10. Charles Sumner Greene, ''Impressions of Some Bungalows and Gardens,'' *The Architect*, 10 (1915): 251–52.

11. Ibid., p. 272, plate 21.

12. ''Tours of Pollyann—Pollyann Finds the Ideal Home Life in Pasadena,'' *Arrowhead* (1917): 21–24.

13. Heineman scrapbooks, Greene and Greene Library, Gamble House.

14. Wilbur David Cook, Jr., ''Highbourne Gardens—a Southern California Bungalow Court, *Architect and Engineer*, 50 (1917): 45.

15. Eugene O. Murmann, *California Gardens* (Los Angeles: published by the author, 1914). The entire book is fascinating, but for the bungalow gardens see especially pp. 61–109.

16. ''Nordoff High,'' *Los Angeles Times*, May 14, 1911, p. 10

17. The bibliography on the ''Social Gospel Movement'' continues to grow as we acknowledge that Christianity, with all its faults, has always had a large minority of aherents who believed that Christ lived to eliminate poverty, cruelty, and injustice. I believe that the best introduction to the movement is still Ralph Henry Gabriel's chapter on it in his *The Course of American Democratic Thought* (New York: The Ronald Press Company, 1940), pp. 256–80.

18. Elsie A. Waggoner, ''The Bungalow Church, a Southland Novelty: New Social Spirit,'' *Los Angeles Times*, Annual Midwinter Number, January 1, 1914, p. 143.

Conclusion

As noted often in the text, the hey-day of bungalow building was in the twenties, though in the main the product was inferior esthetically to the pre-war output. It was also in the twenties that the term *bungalow* began to lose its glamour, in fact to develop derisive connotations. By the thirties the small house was not often built, the depression economy dictating that the building of domestic architecture was the prerogative of the wealthy. The "ranch house" of the forties and fifties had affinities with the bungalow in its identification with a move toward the country, but again the best of the ranch houses were for the well-to-do. The only comparable housing in this period was the tract house with its folksy gabled roof and its inevitable dovecote. In other words, by the late twenties the bungalow and some of the ideas associated with it had become unfashionable. A style of living had become history—except, of course, for the people who lived in bungalows.

The beginning of the bungalow's demise might be found in the looseness of the definition. Randell Makinson, in his book on Charles and Henry Greene, refers to their most lavish mansions as "the ultimate bungalows."[1] He has good precedent for doing so. Charles Greene himself identified the word *bungalow* with the Gamble House and other sumptuous monuments of their style. That Greene would apply the term to objects of beauty that in the first decade of the century cost around $85,000 to build (and today are simply priceless) is an indication that the bungalow had become an idea, signifying any house type that looked as if it had been invented in California—not just the

Twentieth Century Club, 1914; Eagle Rock.

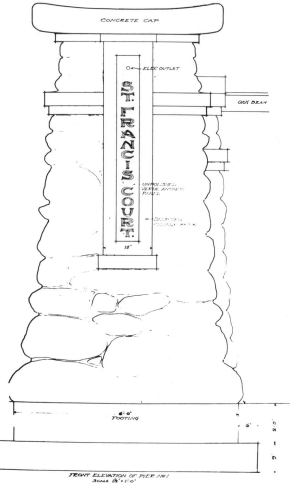

Architect's rendering of gate to St. Francis Court.

original small one-story house. *Bunga-low* meant living in California, close to nature, but also with style. That is what the Gamble House shares with the common bungalow.

But the Greenes were, by their own estimate, uncommon architects. They built a number of houses that could be classed as bungalows by my definition (that is, a one-story house with attic or additional sleeping porch and room), but most of their houses have full second stories. It must be admitted that many other writers also interpreted *bungalow* more broadly to indicate a style of life or especially "Japo-Swiss" characteristics. But with these various loose definitions came a degeneration of the word and the concept. In fact, by the late twenties, popular periodicals printed pictures of the bungalow type but more and more often called them "cottages." The word *bungalow* is dropped except as a term of reproach used in describing the naive little things that had been built in the first three decades of the century.

The entry of bungalow duplexes onto the scene in the twenties was sign of the degeneration of the concept of the single house in its own garden. Duplexes were a very important development for they signaled a change, however slight, in the fabric of life. No matter how cleverly the plan separated the two families in a duplex, the density of population was increasing, even as it had when bungalow courts were erected and even earlier when a second bungalow was built as "income property" in the back yard. The free-standing, single-family dwelling was in trouble because it was an ideal which had difficulty standing up to economic realities. Soon any resemblance to "Broadacre City" was gone, and bungalow areas would be replaced by apartment houses and condominiums that whimsically, nostalgically called themselves "garden" apartments, even if the garden consisted of ersatz turf and plastic geraniums.

The area in Los Angeles just west of Figueroa and north and south of Wilshire is an interesting case in point. The section nearest the central city was rebuilt with apartment houses in the twenties and even earlier. The Depression naturally curtailed building, but when prosperity returned after World War II, apartments began going up and had saturated the area as far as Vermont by the sixties. I recall in 1971 driving my ancient friend, Alfred Heineman, up and down Irolo Street so that he could identify the bungalows and houses he had designed for his brother Arthur's firm. The experience was devastating to me because most of the bungalows were gone, and in their places were stucco fortresses, fairly broadcasting their security systems. Alfred could not have been more amused at the hand of progress sweeping away some of his best designs.

Los Angeles, one of the few cities in America with a reasonably healthy economic growth rate, is not the only scene of bungalow demolition. In all parts of the state, freeways have run through areas of small single-family dwellings. The fact that bungalow developments were largely suburban has actually increased their death rate, since the land they occupy is fair game for builders of freeways and shopping centers.

Yet just as the bungalows seem doomed, they suddenly become attractive to more than a few people. Since the Victorian house has been rehabilitated, not to say worshipped, it was perhaps inevitable that its successor, the Edwardian bungalow, should be rediscovered. Recently a tour of six bungalows in Pasadena attracted over 1,400 viewers with three hundred disappointed and sometimes angry admirers of the bungalow being turned away. Perhaps part of the attraction was the usual one of the now-rare possibility of getting inside other people's houses. But at least one owner of a house on the tour noticed a mood of nostalgia among the tour groups—a longing for the day of the small, homey, mechanically sound bungalow set in a garden under the sun.

Notes
1. Randell Makinson, *Greene and Greene: Architecture as a Fine Art* (Salt Lake City and Santa Barbara: Peregrine Smith, Inc., 1977), pp. 150–87.
2. Charles Sumner Greene, "Bungalows," *Western Architect*, 12 (1908): 3–5.

Bungalow, Arthur S. Heineman (Alfred Heineman, assoc.), 1914; 741 South Irolo, west central Los Angeles, south of Wilshire. Photograph taken July 30, 1979.

Willetts House, Greene and Greene, 1907; 424 Arroyo Terrace, Pasadena. (Greene and Greene Library, Gamble House)

Two Bungalow Apartments.

Spanish Colonial Revival Duplex, ca. 1923, Los Angeles area.

Pueblo Revival Bungalow, 1924; 521 – 12th St., Santa Monica.

Puzzle: Clay Lancaster noticed the similarity of the bungalow at 629 South Grand in Pasadena to a drawing of an ancient Lycian house illustrated in the American Architect and Building News in 1908. If this illustration was the source of his design, John C. Austin, the architect of the bungalow, followed through very quickly, for a picture of it was published in the Western Architect in 1909. In 1910 Henry L. Wilson published a similar design in his Bungalow Book. Wilson's illustration may be a touched up photograph of a very similar bungalow at 990 Vermont in Oakland (see next page), or was the house based on Wilson's design? Related but not so nearly identical bungalows exist in Sierra Madre, Monrovia and probably elsewhere.

Bungalow, Los Robles Court, Arthur S. Heineman (Alfred Heineman, assoc.), 1910; Pasadena. (Greene and Greene Library, Gamble House, Pasadena)

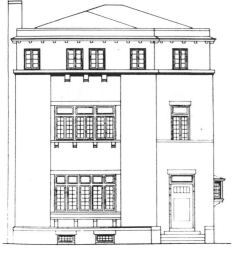

Bungalow ca. 1910. Very similar to the "Urban House" (left) published in the Craftsman, *January, 1905.*

An imposing bungalow in Paso Robles designed, ca. 1910, by James W. Reid. (Comstock, Bungalows, Camps and Mountain Houses, *p. 118.)*

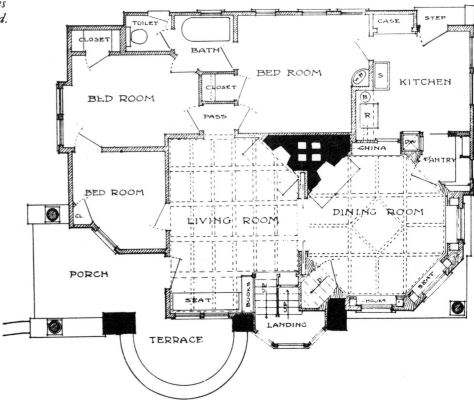

Bungalow, Arthur S. Heineman (Alfred Heineman, assoc.) ca. 1909. Greene and Greene Library, Gamble House, Pasadena)

Thomas House, Sylvanus Marston, 1911; 574 Bellefontaine St., Pasadena.

*Hill House, Walker and Vawter, 1914;
201 South Coronado Street, Los
Angeles.*

Bungalow and View; Vancouver, British Columbia.

Tent bungalow, ca. 1920; used as children's playhouse.

Bungalow, ca. 1921; Uplifters Club Grounds, Pacific Palisades. (Thomas Young)

Bibliographical Note

There are literally no previous books on the history of the bungalow. As for articles, the pioneer investigation was Clay Lancaster's "The American Bungalow," *Art Bulletin*, 40 (September, 1958): 239–53. This was revised and expanded for the same author's *The Japanese Influence in America* (New York City: Walton H. Rawls, 1963), pp. 104–36. The European and Indian origins of the bungalow have been examined by Anthony King in two articles in the British *Architectural Association Quarterly*—"The Bungalow in India: Its Regional and Pre-Industrial Origin," *AAQ*, 5 (1973): 8–26, and "The Bungalow: Social Process and Urban Form," *AAQ*, 5 (1973): 4–21. Whereas Lancaster is most interested in style, King concentrates on social and economic significance.

Reference has been made in the text to the important contemporary articles on the bungalow. As already indicated, the most avid popularizers were the *Craftsman, Ladies Home Journal, House Beautiful, American Architect, Western Architect, Keith's Magazine on Home Building, California Architect and Engineer,* and *International Studio.* But the literature promoting the bungalow was simply tremendous. No newspaper in the period from roughly 1901 to 1925 neglected the latest developments—not only in homes, but also bungalow schools, churches, courts, and gardens.

The central source of information about bungalows comes from the so-called "bungalow books." These were of two kinds: (1) books with few pictures and much text on ideas for interior and exterior decoration and the mechanical systems such as lighting and heating, and (2) books often distributed by the offices of developers or contractors that offered a variety of pictures and floor plans as come-ons for prospective builders. Of the former variety, three stand out: Henry H. Saylor's *Bungalows* (Philadelphia: The

Boulder Bungalow, ca. 1922; Tujunga. A community of about 25 boulder (locally called "cobblestone") bungalows is located at nearby Stonehurst off Sunland Boulevard.

John C. Winston Company, 1911), Henry L. Wilson's *The Bungalow Book* (Chicago: published by the author, 1910), and Charles E. White's *The Bungalow Book* (New York: The Macmillan Company, 1923). These are fairly easy to come by. Much rarer is the second kind, almost never found in libraries. I have assembled my collection largely from secondhand bookstores and have also used similar collections of my friends James and Janeen Marrin and Carol and Kennon Miedema. Often all the details of publication do not appear in the first pages, but I have tried to describe them as closely as possible, even guessing at dates of publication when the styles included seemed to indicate a particular period.

This list, which follows on the next page, is by no means complete. There were literally hundreds of these books.

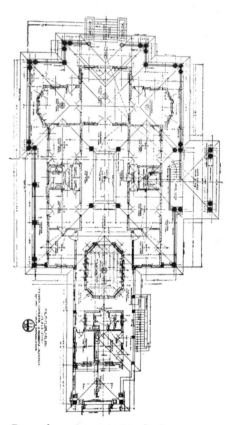

Bungalow, Antonin Nechodoma, ca. 1915; Santurce, Puerto Rico. (Comstock, Bungalows, Camps and Mountain Houses, p. 86.)

Aladdin Homes	(Bay City, Michigan: Aladdin Company, 1919). There were a number of revised editions of this book on prefabricated houses.
Allen Bungalows	(Los Angeles: W. E. Allen Company, 1912).
Cheney, Clyde J.,	*Artistic Bungalows* (Los Angeles: Architectural Construction Company, 1912).
Comstock, William Phillips,	*Bungalows, Camps and Mountain Houses* (New York: the William T. Comstock Co., 1908). A very important book, for it illustrated bungalows throughout the United States and also the work of Antonin Nechodoma, a Prairie Style architect, in Puerto Rico!
The Draughtman Bungalows	(Los Angeles: De Luxe Building Co., 1912).
[Gwynn, Alfred E.],	*A Book of California Bungalows* (Los Angeles: the Alfred E. Gwynn Company, ca. 1912).
Hodgson, Fred T.,	*Practical Bungalows and Cottages for Town and Country* (Chicago: Frederick J. Drake and Company, 1906).
Murmann, Eugene O.	*California Gardens* (Los Angeles: published by the author, 1914)
New Spanish Bungalows	(Los Angeles: the Bungalowcraft Company, 1927).
Radford's Artistic Bungalows	(Chicago and New York: the Radford Architectural Company, 1908).
Standard Building Investment Company Bungalow Book	(Los Angeles and San Diego: the Standard Building Investment Company, ca. 1910).
[Stillwell, E. W.],	*Little Bungalows* (Los Angeles: E. W. Stillwell & Co., 1920).
Stillwell, E. W.,	*Representative California Homes* (Los Angeles: E. W. Stillwell & Co., 1911).
Sweet, Edward E.,	*Sweet's Bungalows* (Los Angeles: Designing and Building Company, ca. 1912).
Telling, George Palmer,	*Select California Bungalows* (Pasadena: 1921).
Weston, Rex D.,	*Weston's Double Bungalows* (Los Angeles: published by author, 1925).
Wilson, Henry,	*America's Modern Homes* (Los Angeles: published by author, ca. 1935). Includes one Streamline Moderne bungalow.

Index

Bungalow, ca. 1920; Kerrisdale, Vancouver, British Columbia.